PRAISES

As a business consultant, I will spend days working out a solid business plan with a client. As we wrap up, he or she is inspired, on fire, and eager to move the plan into reality. Then I'll hop on the plane and as I look out the window, I can almost see the plan dissolve like a sand castle when the tide rolls in. What happens? *FTI...Failure To Implement.*

In his latest book, *FTI*, Howard digs into *why* we self-sabotage and how to move from vision to aligned action to purposeful fulfillment. Howard demonstrates his process with the Ziglar Performance Planner. This powerful planning tool has been around for a while, and you may even have one—just neglected to use it? Howard lovingly shares his approach to success in every area of life and offers love, hope, accountability, community...and results.

ELLEN ROHR
Owner and Franchise Operations Manager of
ZOOM DRAIN Franchising LLC

Howard Partridge hits another home run with *FTI*. This book is for everyone who has, at least once in their lives, failed to do what was needed to maximize the success of an endeavor—personal or professional. It weaves together inspiration, enduring principles of success, practical tools, and access to community support to assist you to achieve and exceed your dreams and aspirations. This is a book for doers on their journey for heightened greatest. Thank you, Howard, for this warm and powerful tool kit.

JOSEPH MICHELLI
Psychologist, Writer, Speaker

Quitting has become an epidemic; people are quitting jobs, marriages, sports, even life. In taekwondo, we say, "A black belt is a white belt that never quit." Failing to implement creates an environment for giving up. You will never have to even think about quitting or giving up when you apply Howard Partridge's 10 Phenomenal Principles that give you the path to accomplish the goals and dreams of your life.

Sr. Grandmaster Brenda J. Sell
World title-holder
"9th-Degree Kukkiwon Black Belt, 1 in 10 million"
President, U.S. Taekwondo
Chung Do Kwan Association
Speaker and Mentor

Howard has a passion for helping people—it is apparent from the first moment you meet him! This book is a labor of love, a guide to help readers overcome the number one reason people and businesses fail: *Failure to Implement*. Each chapter is packed with helpful tools and tips to get past this insidious dream killer. Once you've read and implemented the steps in this book, you will want to share it with your friends, family, and coworkers! Get ready to roll up your sleeves, get some stuff done, and make your dreams come true! Thank you for your body of work, Howard.

Cheri Perry
President, Total Merchant Concepts, Inc.
Washington State Top 100 Places to Work
2017, 2018, 2019

Feel like you are busier than ever? Not seeing the results you expected? I've seen firsthand the phenomenal changes in people's lives and businesses after implementing Howard Partridge's 10 Principles of Phenomenal Performance. They get results—so can you!

Rick Jones
Business Coach and Consultant
Retired President and Owner,
Dale Carnegie Training Center
Houston, Texas

FAILURE TO IMPLEMENT

MORE PHENOMENAL BOOKS BY
HOWARD PARTRIDGE

7 Secrets of a Phenomenal L.I.F.E. (Sound Wisdom 2012)

The 5 Secrets of a Phenomenal Business (Sound Wisdom 2014)

Think and Be Phenomenal: The 5 Levels of Being Phenomenal (Motivational Press 2014)

Phenomenal Marketing Systems: The Fastest Way to the CA$H in Any Business (Sound Wisdom 2015)

Phenomenal SUCCESS Stories: The Simple Path from Survival to Significance (Motivational Press 2017)

Discover Your Phenomenal Dream Life: 17 Principles to Your Phenomenal Destiny (Motivational Press 2017)

The Power of Community: How Phenomenal Leaders Inspire Their Teams, WOW Their Customers, and Make Bigger Profits (McGraw-Hill 2018)

FTI

FAILURE TO IMPLEMENT

The 10 Principles of Phenomenal Performance for Success in Business and Life

HOWARD PARTRIDGE

Published and distributed by:

SOUND WISDOM
P.O. Box 310
Shippensburg, PA 17257-0310
717-530-2122
info@soundwisdom.com
www.soundwisdom.com

Cover/jacket designer: Daena Ciomperlik
Interior designed by Terry Clifton

ISBN 13 HC: 978-1-64095-146-4
ISBN 13 TP: 978-1-64095-148-8
ISBN 13 eBook: 978-1-64095-147-1

For Worldwide Distribution, Printed in the U.S.A.
1 2 3 4 5 6 7 8 / 24 23 22 21 20

DEDICATION

To our beautiful granddaughter Gianna,

Gigi, I had no idea how much love I could have for someone until you came along. I never imagined how much joy I could feel in my heart until I became a grandfather! I discovered what love and joy really is.

Although this book is for everyone, it is especially dedicated to you because Papa wants you to have every advantage possible in life. I want you to be prepared for your phenomenal life, and I want you to be calm and clear in the midst of a confusing and chaotic world.

Papa spent a lifetime learning these simple, but powerful principles, and I now leave them for you. You may never know how much I love you, but I pray that you will:

- Understand your potential—that God made you, and God don't make no junk!

- Have a compelling picture from God of your phenomenal future.

- Know you're here on Earth for a special purpose because God created you for a reason.

- Be surrounded by godly people who love God and who truly love you, and that you'll love others like God loves you.

- Discover God's specific plan for your life.

- Make God your number one priority.
- Follow God's process for living.
- Be productive in God's work every day.

I love you, Gigi!

Papa

ACKNOWLEDGMENTS

To my phenomenal family. No one implements anything meaningful without the loving support of a community. Thank you Denise, Christian, Susy, and Gigi for your love and support.

To my Phenomenal Products Dream Team: Santiago, Michelle, Victoria, Rick, Aliki, Susy, Christian, Ellen Rohr, Cheri Perry, Michelle Prince, and Jim McDonough. Thank you for implementing my ideas, running my companies, and leading our tribe. Our work together is changing lives every day.

To my CAAW Dream Team: Scott, Johann, Juan, Dago, Denise, Kenny, Mary Ann, Jermaine, Laura, Robert, Erika, and all you phenomenal techs and assistants. Thank you for continuing to implement the proven systems day in and day out. I don't see you often, but I love you and brag on you daily.

To Kirby Lammers. Thank you for sharing FTI with me the very first time. These three letters have impacted many people because of you.

To Michelle Prince. Thank you for inspiring me to write about the importance of principles of success.

To our 2 P's in a POD book-writing group. Thank you for giving me valuable feedback on my content.

To our Inner Circle Members. Thank you for being powerful examples of phenomenal implementation! Your success stories inspire me every day!

To Daena Ciomperlik. Thank you for the excellent cover design for this book.

To Tom Ziglar. Thank you for inviting me into the Ziglar world and allowing me to be part of the Ziglar legacy. The Ziglar relationship and partnership has altered my life in profound, powerful, and positive ways. I am forever grateful.

To Alexandra Ziglar. Thank you for implementing my Ziglar projects. There is truly no way I could do my Ziglar work without you. Thank you for your amazing support and your conscientious and impeccable work.

An extra special thanks to Cheri Perry, Rick Jones, Brenda Sell Jones, and Laurie Magers for reviewing this manuscript and making it better than phenomenal!

CONTENTS

Preface 1

Introduction   FTI—Failure To Implement 3

Chapter One   Phenomenal Performance 13

Chapter Two   Phenomenal Principles 27

Chapter Three   Principle 1: The POTENTIAL Principle 47

Chapter Four   Principle 2: The PICTURE Principle 67

Chapter Five   Principle 3: The PURPOSE Principle 83

Chapter Six   Principle 4: The PEOPLE Principle. 101

Chapter Seven   Principle 5: The PLANNING Principle 113

Chapter Eight   Principle 6: The PRIORITY Principle. 125

Chapter Nine   Principle 7: The PROCESS Principle. 139

Chapter Ten   Principle 8: The PRODUCTIVITY Principle 153

Chapter Eleven   Principle 9: The PROGRESS Principle. 167

Chapter Twelve   Principle 10: The PATIENCE Principle. 181

Chapter Thirteen   The POD Principle. 195

Appendix A   13-Week POD Outline. 221

Appendix B   Phenomenal Productivity Books 237

PREFACE

Dear Friend,

I'm not sure what circumstance brought you to this book today, but I want to thank you in advance for reading it. This book represents many hours of writing, thinking, and pushing other important projects aside to get it done.

Once the manuscript was finally finished, I was relieved to have the work completed. It's been a long road. I was also excited, because I know this book will help you no matter where you are in your life or business.

After the last page was written, I walked down to the beach to take a swim. On my way back to the house on the little walkway, a wave of extreme gratitude washed over me. As I looked up to see our beautiful dream home standing proud, I remembered growing up on welfare in a tiny 600 square foot house with a leaky roof in Alabama. Seven kids were crammed into two small bedrooms.

Even more gratitude swept over me as I thought about the amazing experiences I've been blessed to have in my life. I thought about the many challenges God has brought me through.

But most of all, the gratitude swelled up when I thought about all the people God has brought into my life. I've often said, "All of business and all of life is about relationships." I'm completely overwhelmed with the favor I have received from so many people around the world. I'm truly amazed at the number of people who have allowed me into their world.

Now *you* are part of this phenomenal journey. We may or may not know each other yet, but I'm grateful to you for investing your time, money, and energy to learn and to implement the principles of phenomenal performance.

I'm incredibly grateful for the phenomenal life God has granted me. I'm overwhelmingly grateful for my family, my friends, and the freedom to pursue the professional life that I love.

My prayer for you is that *you* would realize *all* of your biggest dreams and goals and that you would experience an incredible amount of joy and fulfillment living out the life God made you to live, and doing the work He has called you to do.

Sincerely,
HOWARD PARTRIDGE
Destin, Florida
October 2019

FTI—FAILURE TO IMPLEMENT
THE NUMBER ONE REASON PEOPLE DON'T REACH THEIR GOALS

Several years ago, I was speaking at a seminar to a group of business owners and sharing that many people have ideas, but they never act on those ideas, and therefore their vision never becomes a reality.

My friend Kirby Lammers was sitting on the front row and muttered "FTI" to the person next to him. "What does that mean?" I asked. "Failure to implement," he responded.

Over the years, I've come to realize that the *number one* reason people don't grow to the next level in their lives, career, or business is FTI, Failure To Implement.

Would you agree that there are things you could do to:

- Have a more successful career or business?
- Be more successful financially?

- Be healthier?
- Have stronger relationships?
- Have more peace?
- Have more hope for the future?
- Have less stress?

Would you agree that many times you simply *don't do* those things?

Would you agree that you don't do things you know you *should* do, even when you know *what* to do and *how* to do them?

Would you like to be more productive?

Would you like to perform at the highest level possible?

Would you like to reach your biggest dreams and goals in life and business?

Of course you would! That's why you picked up this book.

But this is not just a book. It's a guide, and I'm your coach.

This guide reveals 10 powerful principles that will help you become the person you want to be, so you can do the things you want to do, so you can have the life, business, or career you really want.

If you're like most people, you're not fulfilling your God-given potential, and you're not reaching your biggest dreams and goals because of FTI.

One of the most important things I have discovered about FTI is that information alone doesn't create implementation.

In addition to information, you need four more things to consistently implement.

1. *Inspiration.* You'll be inspired by the stories and the quotes in this book. To stay inspired, be sure to download our free resources at www.HowardPartridge.com.

2. *Organization.* As you read the information, you'll want to get yourself organized for maximum implementation. *The Ziglar Personal Performance Planner* is the tool I use to stay focused and organized every day. Get your own planner at www.Ziglar.com.

3. *Training.* As you become aware of the skills you need for maximum performance, you'll want to seek deeper training in areas where you want to perform better.

4. *Community.* Finally, the most important key to implementation is to have the support, encouragement, and accountability from a community of people who care about your success. Join our community at www.HowardPartridgeInnerCircle.com. You can also have your own small group (we call them PODS, which stands for Power Of Discovery Systems.™), to use in your company, church, or service groups. I have provided a 13-week outline at the end of this book that perfectly matches a quarterly schedule.

A couple more things you might want to know before diving into this book:

First, I am a believer in Jesus Christ, so many of my references will come from Scripture. You do not have to be a believer to benefit from these principles, just like you don't need to know Scripture to learn how to ride a bike, but it is my conviction that humans are created by God, and we will not reach our full potential without His presence in our lives. We need the Word of God and the wisdom of God in our lives to navigate our complex, chaotic, and confusing world.

To support the principles I'm sharing with you, I will also share a supporting proverb from the Old Testament Book of Proverbs from time to time. Most of the book was written by King Solomon, who is widely held as the wisest man who ever lived.

Here's what 1 Kings 4:29-34 (ESV) has to say about Solomon: *"And God gave Solomon wisdom and understanding beyond measure, and breadth of mind like the sand on the seashore, so that Solomon's wisdom surpassed the wisdom of all the people of the east and all the wisdom of Egypt. For he was wiser than all other men.... And people of all nations came to hear the wisdom of Solomon, and from all the kings of the earth, who had heard of his wisdom."*

Proverbs contains God's principles that lead to life and wisdom. In fact, Proverbs opens this way: *"The proverbs of Solomon the son of David, king of Israel: To know wisdom and instruction, to discern the sayings of understanding, to receive instruction in wise behavior, righteousness, justice and equity; to give prudence to the naive, to the youth knowledge and discretion, a wise man will hear and increase in learning, and a man of understanding will acquire wise counsel, to understand a proverb and a figure, The words of the wise and their riddles. The fear of the Lord is the beginning of knowledge; Fools despise wisdom and instruction"* (Proverbs 1:1-7 NASB).

Take another look at verse 3: "to receive instruction in *wise behavior."*

Have you ever suffered from *unwise* behavior? I sure have. We all have. Beliefs don't change overnight. Your values change very slowly. It's a journey.

Next, you'll notice I quote a man by the name of Zig Ziglar a *lot.* The first reason is that Zig Ziglar had a profound impact on my life. As we go along in this book, you'll see how influential the Ziglar philosophy has been on my life. This inspirational teacher, the late Zig Ziglar, touched an estimated quarter-of-a-billion lives through his speeches, books, and recordings.

Zig was one of the most influential public speakers in the world, and certainly became a legend in the American landscape. To this day, he is most likely the most quoted motivational speaker on Earth. Our hurting world needs this message of hope and encouragement today more than ever before.

Second, the Ziglar philosophy is a complete philosophy for personal and professional performance. Why would I recreate the wheel when it's already complete?

Third, I have personally witnessed many of the lives that have been transformed by the Ziglar philosophy, which incidentally is also based on the Word of God as well.

Fourth, keeping the Ziglar legacy alive is now part of my professional role. Over the past eight years since Zig Ziglar spoke on my stage, I became the exclusive small business coach for Ziglar, Inc. Later I was honored to become the world's first *Ziglar Legacy Certified Trainer.* That was followed by an offer to become Executive Vice President of Training Operations, which I was thrilled to accept.

Today, I help Tom Ziglar run the company, which I could not do without Tom's daughter, Alexandra Ziglar. I try not to miss an opportunity to recognize Alexandra because she serves me so well in my role at Ziglar. She is extremely conscientious, and her work is impeccable. She is super smart and fun to work with. Who better to help us bring the Ziglar message into the future than a young and talented Ziglar!

The icing on the cake of working with Ziglar is all of the wonderful people around the world I have the pleasure of meeting. Recently, my wife and I visited one of the Ziglar Legacy Certified Trainers at her home in Rome, as we capped off a two-week trip to Italy. My passion for you is to have phenomenal success in all areas of your personal and professional life. The Word of God and the Ziglar philosophy are two main sources I rely on.

Finally, if you have read any of my other seven books, you may notice that I have repeated a story, a concept, or an illustration that appears in a previous book. That's because this book you are now reading ties all of my previous books together. From *7 Secrets of a Phenomenal L.I.F.E.* to *The 5 Secrets of a Phenomenal Business,* to *Think and Be Phenomenal,* to *Phenomenal Marketing Systems,* to *Phenomenal Success Stories,* to *Discover Your Phenomenal Dream Life,* to *The Power of Community,* they all require implementation. That's the purpose of this book—to help you implement the things that are important to you, so you can reach your biggest dreams and goals in life and business.

Again, this is not just a book. It's a growth journey that should continue long after you read the book. I want to personally challenge you to live by the *10 proven* principles that will drive the performance you desire. Each of the principles is followed by a very important question.

1. **The POTENTIAL Principle:** *Understanding Your Potential Impacts Phenomenal Performance.* "Who do you think you are?" All humans suffer from a poor self-image to one degree or another. Who you think you are, and Whose you think you are will determine whether you act on your goals or not?

2. **The PICTURE Principle:** *A Compelling Picture Imagines Phenomenal Performance.* "Where are you going?" Human beings do what they see in their minds. This can be positive or negative. If you can't see yourself doing something, you won't even try. But when you have a clear picture in your mind, and you believe it, you will take the steps to get there. You have to see the reaching of your goals in your mind first.

3. **The PURPOSE Principle:** *Knowing Your Purpose Inspires Phenomenal Performance.* "Why do you do what you do?" Humans are created for a purpose, but most people never find their purpose. Many live lives that are meaningless, just getting through the stress of the day. Knowing your purpose gives you a new level of energy and passion.

4. **The PEOPLE Principle:** *The Right People Influence Phenomenal Performance.* "Who do you have around you?" The people you have around you will either keep you from being productive or promote your potential and purpose. Your closest friends, family, and associates heavily influence you, whether you admit it or not. Having the right people around you will help you understand your potential, to help you see a more meaningful picture, and help you embrace your purpose.

5. **The PLANNING Principle:** *Proper, Focused Planning Initiates Phenomenal Performance.* "How will you get there?" You can't go somewhere you've never been without a map. When you have the right directions, you can get where you are going faster and easier. You cannot even get started without an itinerary!

6. **The PRIORITY Principle:** *Living by Priority Ignites Phenomenal Performance.* "What's important now?" Life offers many opportunities, both good and bad. That's why it is so easy to get distracted. Staying focused on what's truly important every day is key to long-term implementation.

7. **The PROCESS Principle:** *A Simple Process Improves Phenomenal Performance.* "What systems will you use?" Creating simple systems into your life and business makes production more predictable and precise, which saves you time, energy, and money.

8. **The PRODUCTIVITY Principle:** *Consistent, Persistent Productivity Insures Persistent, Consistent.* "What action are you taking?" We know we need to be more productive to reach goals we have not reached before, but the kind of action we take each day is critical. We need to take *focused* action *every* day that takes us closer to the goal. How you use your time each day is vital to phenomenal performance.

9. **The PROGRESS Principle:** *Tracking Your Progress Illuminates Phenomenal Performance.* "How are you tracking?" Just like tracking your progress on a trip, you need to track your performance so you know how you are progressing. Are you early? Late? Right on time? Tracking your success reveals (illuminates) your performance, good or bad.

10. **The PATIENCE Principle:** *Exercising Great Patience Increases Phenomenal Performance.* "What will you give?" Reaching a level of phenomenal performance doesn't happen overnight, it happens over *time.* The Patience Principle helps you live these principles for the long haul. Diligence over time brings huge rewards.

Each of the chapters are followed with the Action Steps required to implement the information shared more effectively.

ACTION STEPS

1. Get my free training that will inspire you to implement at www.HowardPartridge.com. Every week, you will receive free training to help you perform better in your personal life and in business.

2. Get your *Ziglar Personal Performance Planner* at www.Ziglar.com. The Ziglar Planner is the tool our members use to stay focused and to track our goals. I will reference the planner in every chapter.

3. Join a *Growth POD* at www.HowardPartridgeInnerCircle .com. A Growth POD is a small group where you receive support, encouragement, and accountability

CHAPTER ONE

PHENOMENAL PERFORMANCE

The Inspired Person **INVITES** Phenomenal Performance

WHY DON'T WE IMPLEMENT?

So, why don't we implement, even when we know *what* to do and *how* to do it? *Why* do we not do the things we *know* are going to help us reach our goals? *Why* do we self-sabotage? *Why* do we keep doing the same thing over and over, somehow hoping for different results?

I've spent the past twenty-five years thinking about these questions, and the past two decades observing the reasons for FTI while coaching business owners, leaders, and individuals to succeed.

There are plenty of books on productivity available, but if we don't understand *why* we fail to implement, we won't reach our most important goals. We can have all the books in the world, and all the productivity apps in the world, but they will not help us unless we understand *why* we don't implement.

Zig Ziglar said, "The secret ingredient of success is desire, and desire comes from a vision." If desire is the secret ingredient and the result of a vision, *why* don't more people have a compelling vision for their life? And if they have a vision, why don't they work harder to make that vision a reality?

I think everyone understands that if we want to reach our biggest dreams and goals, we have to perform at a higher level. I call that *phenomenal* performance. Extraordinary, amazing performance leads to bigger and better results. We all know that—so why do we not perform at the highest level possible?

Is it a lack of:

- Time?
- Focus?
- Discipline?
- Motivation?

Everyone has the same amount of time, but some use their time more wisely than others. The question is *why?* Anyone who wants to accomplish more certainly can see the value in being more focused, but *why* do we lack focus? A common lament is, "I need to be more disciplined"; but *why* do we lack discipline? Motivation is important too, but *why* do we lack motivation?

People tend to make extraordinary changes in their lives and business only out of *desperation* or *inspiration*. Desperation occurs when we are faced with a looming situation that will cause a great deal of pain—we have to pay a crucial bill, or we have a health scare. Or maybe, we have had a big argument with someone we love and the relationship is on the line. If there is no reconciliation, that relationship may be lost forever.

In the desperation scenario, the pain has to be great enough to cause us to change. Many people won't change because they feel that making a change will be more painful than their current situation.

Humans can sometimes be like the old farmer's hound dog. The farmer was sitting on the porch in his rocking chair, his hound dog lying next to him. The mailman approached to deliver the mail and noticed that the hound was moaning in pain. "What's the matter with your dog, mister?"

"I think he's lying on a nail" responded the farmer.

"Well, why don't he get up?" the mailman wondered out loud.

"I guess it don't hurt bad enough," the farmer assumed.

A few years ago, I was in Australia on a five-city seminar tour, and the sponsor took me to a cricket match in Perth. As I was walking along, I noticed an empty, discarded cigarette pack on the ground. It had disgusting pictures of what a smoker's lungs look like. I learned that some countries, like Australia, require tobacco manufacturers to put gruesome photographs on their packages to remind people of the dangers of smoking.

Being curious about human nature, and a little bold, I picked up the empty pack and walked up to a couple of young chaps who were smoking at the cricket match and asked them how they felt about the photos on the package. They just shrugged their shoulders and made a joke about it.

The problem with changing through desperation is that as soon as we get back into our comfort zone, we tend to relax. Then we are vulnerable to slip back into desperation mode, and the cycle continues. Can you relate to that in any areas of your life or business?

Desperation may motivate us for a bit, but it wears off as soon as we get comfortable again. The bigger problem is that we tend to make poor decisions when we are led by desperation. These decisions may solve our immediate problem but cause serious problems later on.

Desperation is one form of "external" motivation. A negative situation motivates people to take massive action. But external motivation can come from a positive source as well. For example, you're motivated to get a lot of things done so you can go on vacation, or you're motivated to make a sale to get a bonus.

But external motivation isn't enough for long-term, sustained implementation. What we really need is *internal* motivation, or better known as *inspiration*. Inspiration comes from an internal source. Inspiration happens when a fire is ignited inside us. Inspiration is created by a vision so powerful and meaningful that it cannot be easily extinguished.

Inspiration creates a burning desire so hot and so compelling that we put our entire mind, will, and emotion into making the vision a reality. Inspiration happens when the lights finally go on. I was visiting a friend, and he was telling me about his "checkered" past. He had been in jail for about a year, and somehow, seemingly out of the blue, his internal lights went on. He said he knew he would be okay even if he didn't get out of jail right away.

When the lights of inspiration come on, there is no stopping you. But even as powerful as inspiration is, humans need something even bigger than inspiration. We need the answer to these questions:

- *Why* do we fail to implement even when we know we could reach our biggest dreams and goals?

- *Why* do fail to implement even when we know what to do?

- *Why* do we fail to implement even when it really hurts us and others?

- *Why* do fail to implement the things we *know* will take our business or career to the next level?

- *Why* do we not live out the spiritual life we really want to experience?

Long-term, sustainable implementation comes down to one thing—our *beliefs.*

Deep down, we don't *believe* that we can reach the vision, or that we should pursue it. If we are honest with ourselves, we don't truly *believe* the effort will be worth the reward. People don't do the things they really need to do to get what they really want, because deep down, they don't *believe* the vision will come true. They don't *believe* the prize will be worth the fight.

While it's true that a lack of focus, feeling overwhelmed, poor habits, lack of organization, and or training come into play, they are all just symptoms. If you don't *believe* there will be a big payoff, internally or externally, you won't wake up inspired to do the hard work required to reach your greatest dreams and goals. You won't sustain implementation over a long period of time without *believing in the successful end result.*

The reason I wrote this book is because I have seen these principles work time and time again.

I started my first business out of the trunk of my car thirty-five years ago. Over thirteen long years, I became a slave to my business, working twenty hours a day, seven days a week. I was a demanding boss and the handful of employees I had were under a lot of pressure and worked ridiculously long hours as well. Plus, my business was in major debt.

So, how did I transform that business into a multimillion dollar, predictable, profitable, turnkey business, that I now don't even have to work at? By *doing* things differently. I learned and *implemented* better financial systems. I learned and *implemented* better leadership practices. I learned and *implemented* systems in all areas of my business. As a result, I enjoy the proceeds of a profitable and growing business without having to work *in* it myself. It's truly a blessing.

For the past two decades, I've been helping other small business owners, leaders, and individuals reach their wildest dreams and greatest goals in life and in business. My most successful students are those who simply learn the systems and *implement* them. Over the past eight years working with Ziglar,

I've seen countless people grow as a result of simply *implementing* the Ziglar philosophy.

As for myself, the result of implementing the proven principles helped me become a best-selling author and an international business coach, which has helped me help many others. I never could have imagined the lives that are being transformed through the work we do.

When Mr. Ziglar was with us in person, he opened many of his speeches with the following question: "How many of you believe that there are things you can do in the next two weeks that would make your personal life or business life *worse?*"

That always got the audience's attention. He would then say, "Then it stands to reason that there are things you can do to make your personal life or business life *better,* and the choice is yours."

My wife, Denise, and I have been married for thirty-five years, and I can tell you for *sure* there were things I did and did *not* do that caused my marriage to be better or worse! If you're married, or in any kind of relationship, I don't have to tell you about that!

It turns out that even love itself comes down to implementation. You see, I can tell my wife I love her, but I have to *show* her that I love her. Have you ever heard that love is a verb? That love is action? Thirty-five years of marriage have shown me this is true.

Even a person's walk with God is shaped by what we do or don't do. Now, as a believer in Jesus Christ, I believe what *He* did saves our souls, but we have to take the *action* to accept

His gift. After we become believers, our *position* in Christ is secure, but what we do or don't do definitely affects our *condition*. There are things we can *do* to help us build a stronger relationship with God and improve our condition.

At one time, I was terribly unhealthy. You might say I was the proverbial "walking heart attack." I ate the wrong things at the wrong times, and I didn't exercise. I was overweight, lethargic, and had awful migraine headaches that caused excruciating pain from the top of my head to the tip of my toes. In fact, the headaches would make me so sick I could barely walk.

One of these episodes occurred during a trip to Holland. As my wife and I were touring the tulip fields, I got so sick I was doubled over on the sidewalk. A Dutchman pulled over and asked if we needed help. "Yes, we need a doctor!" Denise shouted back. "Follow me!" he responded hastily.

I crawled into the passenger seat of the rental car and Denise followed the man as he led us to a doctor's office. After he pointed out his window at a tiny white cottage with a front porch, surrounded by manicured greenery, he drove off.

As we approached the house-made doctor's office, the sign on the front door revealed that it was a veterinarian clinic! But because of socialized medicine in that country, the animal doctor was able to treat me with some pills that really worked! I'm probably the only person you know who has been medically treated by a Dutch vet!

How did I get healthy and get rid of the headaches? By *doing* something different. By eating differently. By *implementing* a health plan.

A few years ago, I was coaching a married couple who owned a business. They were on the brink of divorce because of a lack of income in the business. They actually had enough sales, but they weren't billing the clients in a timely manner to invoice to the insurance company.

It was the husband's role in the business to make sure the insurance companies were billed, but there were several steps in building the client file, so he simply didn't get it done in a timely manner.

Before the couple got married, the wife had stellar credit, but since the business wasn't collecting the money it was owed, the personal bills became delinquent and her credit was affected, which made her very angry.

As I got into the coaching session and began to unpack the problems, I eventually asked the obvious question "So, what you're telling me is that if you simply fix the invoicing problem, all these other problems go away?" They both agreed it was that simple.

I'm sure you can already see the solution as easily and as clearly as I did: GET THE INVOICES OUT! Why couldn't the husband see this as clearly as I did? Why is it that people will allow something as simple as that to affect their business so dramatically that it could destroy their marriage?

As we drilled down into the problem, he shared that there were several steps his team needed to take before the invoice could be created. We created a simple process, and he committed to implementing the procedures.

Why did he let a business problem like that continue to fester when he knew it was destroying his business and marriage? You could ask the same question about an addict.

To everyone looking in from the outside, you can easily see how alcoholics or drug addicts could turn their lives around. Stop drinking. Stop doing drugs. But it isn't that easy. In fact, FTI is an addiction just like anything else. We are addicted to our habits regardless how destructive they are. We are emotionally tied to them, and our culture doesn't make it easy to change.

Just like alcoholics or drug addicts, we need a recovery program. The solution for this man was simple. It just wasn't easy for him. I created some easy procedures for him, and the good news is he *did* implement the solution and as a result saved his business and his marriage.

It's great that he took action, but here's another FTI warning: Once sober, it's easy for addicts to fall back into their old ways. Many years ago, after being terribly unhealthy, I got super fit. I maintained my super-healthy lifestyle for eight years.

Then something happened. I stopped doing some of the things that made me healthy. I began to slip back into some of my old habits. The result is that I am not as healthy as I once was. Fortunately, I'm still healthy and I don't get migraines any longer, but I'm not *super* fit like I was before.

Over the past two decades of coaching small business owners, leaders, and individuals, I have seen thousands of examples of how FTI has kept them from reaching their full potential. The solution is usually a simple one, but many individuals seem hopelessly tied to poor habits. And I venture to say that most people have at least one area in their life or career where they struggle the most.

Performance is key. Whether that means eating and exercising, loving someone, or reaching your sales goals, the better we perform, the better outcome we will have. But in order to achieve phenomenal performance, we have to be able to *see* and *believe* the possibilities.

Is it possible to be successful in all areas of life? Is it possible to be healthy, wealthy, *and* wise in today's fast-paced world? Is it possible to win in every area of business? The answer is a resounding *yes!* I've seen thousands of examples, and I've had an abundance of experiences in both failure and success myself. I've led many people in many industries in many countries and in many walks of life improve their lives and business by implementing simple systems. As your coach, I'll try to help you as well.

For now, let's understand that our behavior—implementation—is simply a result of our beliefs. Discovering what is underneath the surface is a worthy, lifelong endeavor, and seeing false beliefs changed is exciting indeed!

The *truth* will set you free. Once the lights go on and you see the truth—that you *can* reach your fondest dreams and goals in life—you'll be inspired to perform.

ACTION STEPS

1. Put your contact information in your *Ziglar Personal Performance Planner*. Remember that you will use the planner as your constant companion, so make sure you order it if you haven't already.

2. Fill in the *Personal Commitment* on page 1 of the planner. By making a commitment, you are saying you believe in your future success!

3. Participate in your weekly POD. If you are not in a POD yet, go to www.HowardPartridgeInnerCircle .com to enroll.

The secret ingredient of success is desire, and desire comes from a vision.
—ZIG ZIGLAR

Hope deferred makes the heart sick, but desire fulfilled is a tree of life.
—PROVERBS 13:12 ESV

The thoughts of the righteous are just; the counsels of the wicked are deceitful.
—PROVERBS 12:5 ESV

The blessing of the Lord brings wealth, without painful toil for it.
—PROVERBS 10:22 NIV

Our behavior is simply a result of our beliefs.
—HOWARD PARTRIDGE

CHAPTER TWO

PHENOMENAL PRINCIPLES

Adopting Positive Principles **INTENSIFIES** Phenomenal Performance

WHAT DO YOU BELIEVE?

After Zig Ziglar spoke at my conference, I got to know his son, Tom Ziglar. Tom invited me to present a series of live videos from their studio. The host of the show was a positive, energetic, lovely woman by the name of Michelle Prince. Michelle and I hit it off, and I was invited back for several more episodes. Michelle had been positively impacted by Zig Ziglar when she was only seventeen years old, and eventually worked at Ziglar.

Each time I saw Michelle, we began to share our vision of spreading the Ziglar message to more people. We found that we had similar passions, and it seemed we were always thinking about the same things. We even created very similar content without the other knowing about it.

Michelle and I were both in the first Ziglar Legacy Certification course, and as my role grew with Ziglar, Michelle and I began sharing the stage more and more. She now emcees all of my conferences. People often say we are like two peas in a pod. Michelle helps authors write and publish books, and we have a coaching group for authors that we lead together. The name of the group is 2 P's in a POD. Prince and Partridge are the two P's, and a POD is my small group format. Get it? Corny I know, but it's fun.

Michelle was teaching at Ziglar Legacy Recertification one day on her *PRINCE-IPLES of Success*, a play on her name of course. As she began sharing the principles, I realized that we were both working on a similar message. Michelle's principles reminded me that implementation is simply a result of the *principles* we live by.

What you *believe* determines the *principles* you live by. In other words, there are principles each of us live by that determine what we *do* or don't do. The guiding principles we live by either serve us well or they don't.

An even better word for belief is *faith*.

Faith is more than believing in our head that something will work. It's a deep conviction in a future outcome, even when there is no evidence for it. Faith is the belief that planting and watering *will* reap a harvest.

Faith produces powerful visions and a peace that the vision will come true. *Faith* engages your spirit, soul, and body in a way that causes you to take massive action even in the midst of fear. Fear is the enemy of faith and the cause of stress. Fear and doubt kill more dreams than anything else.

Does that mean we should just have blind faith and throw caution to the wind? Of course not. Faith must be mixed with action. Jesus Himself said, "Therefore, I say to you, all things for which you pray and ask, believe that you have received them, and they will be granted you" (Mark 11:24 NASB).

There are a couple of key words in this passage: "pray and ask," that's doing something. "Believe that you have received them," that's called faith. When faith is mixed with wisdom and the support of the right people, you can accomplish all that God has for you to accomplish.

In the Old Testament story of the Exodus, the children of Israel wandered the desert for forty years and didn't enter the promised land because of unbelief. Just outside their grasp was a land "flowing with milk and honey." Meanwhile, they were griping about the manna that fell from heaven every day as food. They were complaining about the miracle that was keeping them alive! They had experienced the Red Sea being opened for them and watched God manifest Himself through a pillar of smoke by day and a pillar of fire by night to direct them.

How could they not believe after all of that?

Because their fear was greater than their faith. Their doubt was bigger than the dream. They were afraid of the people they had to fight. Their lack of belief created a negative attitude, and they chose to stay in the desert rather than take the land, even though they were told they would win.

Eventually, Joshua, a man of faith, led them into the promised land, but not until the first generation of unbelievers died off.

This story is a powerful illustration of what happens in our own souls. The promised land represents our dreams and goals, or in a strict spiritual sense, the salvation of our souls. The land is our soul—our mind, will, and emotion. We must conquer the land in order to experience all God has for us.

Instead of mixing our thinking with faith, we allow fear to enter into our emotions, keeping us from the promise. We don't allow ourselves to *believe* that we can reach the promised land, or we begin to fear that it isn't even real. It's just a mirage. Our beliefs change when we change our thinking. We change our thinking with the input into our minds. One of the most powerful things to put in our mind is the fact that someone else has already done what we want to do. We see the change in their lives, and we are inspired by it.

When we have faith that we can overcome the obstacles we see, our emotions change. Emotion is a powerful force. Whether the emotion is positive or negative, whether it's a burning desire or a feeling of fear, emotions drive action.

So, how do we maintain positive emotions like love and resist negative emotions like fear? With truth. Through wisdom. Your beliefs are changed through your thinking. And your thinking is changed by putting the truth in your mind. Zig Ziglar famously said, "You are what you are and where you are because of what has gone into your mind. You can change what you are and where you are by changing what goes into your mind."

Fear is overcome by faith. Fear is overcome by truth. Our culture today is driven by media that feeds us a constant diet of fear and entertainment that produces an unhealthy sense of pride, which is a product of fear.

We are created as spirit, soul, and body. Our soul contains our mind, will, and emotion. Our emotion says, "Hey, I want ice cream." Our mind says, "If you want to be healthy, don't eat ice cream." Who's going to win this battle? The late psychologist Dr. Bill Gillham taught in his southern Oklahoma drawl that "Big Will is gonna win every time!"

How do you change your will to respond to the truth? We need support. We must have community. We must have someone in our life who is going to hold us accountable and say, "Do you really want to be healthy? Do you really believe that you're going to be healthy?"

Our hidden emotional and limiting beliefs come from fear at some level. Fear that comes directly from our negative emotions tells us fantastic lies. Do you know the widely held acronym for F.E.A.R. is False Evidence Appearing Real? You see, God gave us a phenomenal imagination to create life. But sometimes we use it in all the wrong ways.

As you're attempting to change your habits, the lies come up again and again that say you'll never make it. It's a lie and your mind must confess the truth. The truth is you *can* do it. There's an old story about an Indian brave who confessed to the chief that he felt like there were two wolves inside him. One was good and one was bad. "Which one will win?" he asked the wise chief. "The one you feed," he responded. The two wolves are named Faith and Fear.

An exercise I discovered along the way that I've found helpful in dealing with internal dialogue is called the *Fear Behind the Fear*. The exercise is all about asking what's the fear behind each fear you can identify. Then, replacing the lie with the truth and confessing the truth.

Here's an example. I was coaching a business owner who didn't want to go out and make referral source marketing visits. Referral Source Marketing is the most powerful marketing strategy we teach. With this system, you visit business owners who have the clients you want to do business within their circle of influence.

I was holding this business owner accountable to make these visits on a phone session, and she finally confessed that she was afraid to go out and make them.

"What are you afraid of?" I asked.

"I'm afraid they won't like me."

What's the fear behind that?"

"They won't refer me."

"What's the fear behind that?" I pressed.

"Then I won't be able to pay my bills," she said with a new level of intensity.

"Okay, what's the fear behind that?"

"If they don't refer me, I won't be able to feed my kids!" she finally burst out.

Wow! Isn't it amazing how hidden fears can take us so far down a destructive road? And we aren't even aware of it! That's *false evidence appearing real!*

I then began to coach her toward the truth. What's the truth? The truth is that she wasn't visiting any of these people anyway. They weren't referring her anyway! So, I asked her a few more questions:

"Let me get this straight. You're not calling on any of these people right now?"

"Right."

"Okay, so they're not referring you right now?"

"Right."

"Are you still making money in your business?"

"Yes."

"As long as you've been in business, as long as you've had kids, have you always paid your bills?"

"Yes."

"Have your kids always had something to eat?"

"Of course, they have."

She got it. This was FEAR (False Evidence Appearing Real) *lying* to her!

The next step in the coaching call was to use that same imagination to think about what *could* happen. Back to our conversation to drill down on the *possibilities*.

"There's not a credible reason that they wouldn't like you, right?" I asked.

"No," she admitted.

"And even if they didn't like you and they didn't refer you, they're not going to go onto the Internet and post that you're a terrible person for bringing them cookies, right?"

"Of course not," she continued to admit.

My closing argument was,

"What *could* happen if you *did* make those calls and you made them *consistently?* What could happen if you did the referral calls the best they could be done?"

Because of this session, that business owner went on to create some amazing referral partners and added thousands of dollars to her business.

When we mix our God-given desires with a sound mind, we can create a more meaningful vision for our lives and for our work. Wisdom creates the right thinking and beliefs that result in the right actions.

God says to the believer, "I have not given you a spirit of fear, but of love and power and of a sound mind." Wisdom comes from saturating yourself in truth, prayer, and surrounding yourself with the right people—community. My training and coaching company, Phenomenal Products, was founded on Proverbs 15:22 that says, "Without consultation, plans are frustrated. But with many counselors, plans succeed."

Our modern culture is so bent on being independent that we miss out on the wisdom and experience of others. Sure, many people have received bad advice and have been taken advantage of by others, but that doesn't mean you can't find the right coach, consultant, or community who can help you reach your goals.

How and when do belief systems begin? A positive belief system begins when you realize your phenomenal potential because you know who you are and *Whose* you are. It continues when the lights go on and you see a preferred future for your life and career. And it really gets strong when you find your purpose—the reason you were even born! It continues when you place the right people around you who will help you live by faith.

On the other hand, limiting belief systems come from a number of causes. Some beliefs are conditioned beliefs. In other words, as you grew up you were conditioned to believe certain things. You were conditioned to believe certain things about God, others, yourself, money, relationships, work, life, and many other things. You may not have even been taught them, but you caught them.

Maybe your limiting beliefs exist because you don't feel worthy of your calling. Moses had that problem. He had to have his brother, Aaron, speak for him. Maybe you don't believe you deserve success. Maybe you believe that you don't have the skills and training to reach the goal you really want to reach. Maybe you have hidden emotional beliefs that create unknown fears. Maybe you've been conditioned your entire life to believe a certain thing, and you've never taken the time to discover for yourself what the truth really is. Maybe you've been conformed to the general worldview by the media that you have to be something or someone else to be acceptable to society.

Everyone has their own set of beliefs. Everyone has their own belief about God, others, and themselves. Humans are creatures of habit, and most of the action you take every day, or don't take, is simply a result of what's happening below the surface.

Imagine an iceberg for a moment. Maybe only 10 percent of the ice is visible of the water. That represents your conscious mind. But 90 percent is hidden underneath the water. This represents your subconscious mind working below the surface of your awareness. This is where your true beliefs, emotions, habits, and values reside. You are being driven by your subconscious mind! You've probably heard that before. You've probably also heard or learned that you can change your subconscious mind with your conscious mind. You do that by putting in the pure, the powerful, and the positive into your mind.

We will never get to the bottom of our hidden beliefs as long as we live, but we can check our beliefs, how we think and feel, and we can test them against the truth. The fact is that our subconscious minds, our subconscious beliefs, have been built over our lifetime, so it will take time to become the pure, positive, productive person we want to be.

Those beliefs—even if they are limiting beliefs, emotional beliefs, conditioned beliefs, or hidden beliefs—will always operate consistently whether you consciously think about them or not. The key to phenomenal performance is to live by principles that are *proven* to drive the performance that will deliver positive results.

DISCLAIMER: If an individual has a strong addiction or mental condition, professional counseling, a medical solution, or spiritual intervention may be required to break free. This book is written for those who can critically think about their current situation and bring awareness to what's happening in their lives. I am not a counselor and I am not a doctor. Even though these principles may or may not help you with long-term addictions, I've seen them practiced by thousands of people over the past two decades, and they have helped me as well.

PROMISES

As a believer in Christ, there are many promises God has given us to live enjoyable lives. Our belief in these promises determines the principles we live by and the philosophy we hold. My pastor, Neil McClendon, recently preached on the subject of Promise. He shared these promises of Christ:

- He promises to be with us in our darkest times (Psalm 23:4).

- He promises to give us wisdom if we ask (James 1:5).

- He promises that in all things He is at work (Romans 8:28).

- He promises to provide a way out of temptation (1 Corinthians 10:13).

- He promises that as Christians we are forgiven forever (Hebrews 10:8-14).

- He promises that our salvation is secure, no matter what (John 10:28-29).

- He promises that He is not put off by our weaknesses (2 Corinthians 12:8-10).

- He promises to never leave us nor forsake us (Hebrews 13:5).

- He promises to return (John 14:3).

PEACE

When you know God and His promises and you accept them, you will have peace. What you believe changes your perspective. Few stories demonstrate this fact more than the story of Horatio Spafford. Spafford was a very successful lawyer and businessman in Chicago. The infamous Chicago fires ruined him financially, so he decided to move his family to Europe. At the last minute, he had to stay behind for a zoning issue concerning the fire and his property. He sent his wife and four daughters ahead. Their ship collided with another ship and sunk, and he lost all four of his daughters in that tragic accident. His wife survived. As soon as he received the telegraph from his wife, he boarded a ship to go and meet her in Europe.

During his trip across the Atlantic, the captain of the ship came to him and pointed out the area where the accident took place. Spafford, after surveying the scene, immediately went to his cabin and penned the words to the now-famous hymn *It Is Well with My Soul*. The hymn begins with these words:

> *When peace like a river attendeth my way,*
> *When sorrows like sea billows roll,*
> *Whatever my lot, Thou hast taught me to say*
> *It is well, it is well, with my soul.*

Honestly, I cannot imagine dealing with such a tragedy as what happened to this man and his wife, but his perspective came from how he viewed God's promises. Fortunately, that was not the end of Spafford's story. Not only has the hymn inspired millions, he and his wife had three more daughters and ended up creating a mission in Jerusalem that has served many, many people around the world for many, many years.

PROCLAMATION

Since the reason we don't implement is a lack of faith, I would like to offer a simple way to build your faith. That tip is to simply *confess* the truth. The truth is that you *can* reach the vision you have. Remember that your belief changes as a result of what you think about, and your thinking is changed by what you put into your mind.

Proclaiming the truth ingrains belief. Confessing who you are, what you can do, and what God says about you is the key. When you understand what the truth is, confess it *verbally*. Prayer is very powerful. Ask God to give you faith.

The key is to visualize who you are becoming in present tense. *I AM* are the two most powerful words in the English language. The fact is that we are what we are and who we are because of what has gone into our mind. We can change what we are and where we are by changing what goes into our mind. As we intentionally do that, our conscious mind retrains our subconscious mind. Our true values are shown by what we do. We do what we value, we value what we do. It's as simple as that.

Confess the truth of who you are and Whose you are. Confess the truth about what you can accomplish. You may not feel the belief, but that doesn't mean it's not true. Feelings are not facts. What is the *truth* about reaching your goals? The truth is that you *can* reach those goals because you are already the person you need to be and you already have the qualities of success you need. We will cover this in detail in the next chapter.

Ziglar has an Affirmation Card for you to verbalize your confessions of who you are becoming every morning and every night. As you read this card aloud and look yourself in the eye in the mirror, you begin to train your subconscious mind to believe it, and therefore you obtain those qualities. I have seen this process alone change many individuals. Jim and Lori Ellis, members of our book-writing group, just finished a manuscript of affirmations from Scripture. I am so excited to read it and to *confess* those Scriptures!

POSITION

We must live out of our *position* rather than our condition. When we proclaim our position, we say things like:

- I AM born to win, designed for accomplishment, engineered for success, and endowed with the seeds of greatness. After all, God don't make no junk!

- I AM a phenomenal product, created to be phenomenal, to do phenomenal things, and to have a phenomenal life!

- I AM born to win; but in order be the winner I was born to be, I must *plan* to win and *prepare* to win before I can *expect* to win. And when I *plan* to win and *prepare* to win, I can *expect* to win!

That's what the *10 Principles of Phenomenal Performance* are all about. Helping you *plan* to win and to *prepare* to win!

PHILOSOPHY

The principles that you believe in—what you really and truly *believe*—produce your philosophy of life. Having a solid philosophy of life and business is really important. Once you have a true philosophy that works, you simply have to manage it each day.

If someone observed you, what would they say your philosophy is in each area of life? For example, if someone observed my financial life when I was in major credit card debt, they would correctly say that I believe in debt. Today, they would clearly say my philosophy of life is a debt-free philosophy.

What is your philosophy about your health? About family? About business? About your career? It's not what you *say* you believe, but what you actually *do* that is the real truth. The fact is that we already have a philosophy about each and every one of these areas of life, whether they are working for us or not. We all have a philosophy of life whether we are aware of it or not.

When we become aware of what's happening, we can then change our thinking about these areas. Then we can change the input to change our thinking. When we change our thinking, we change our beliefs. When we change our beliefs, we change our expectations. When we change our expectations, we change our attitude. When we change our attitude, we change our behavior. When we change our behavior, we change our performance. When we change our performance, we change our life for the better!

You may recognize the following words of wisdom attributed to Frank Outlaw: "Watch your thoughts; they become words. Watch your words; they become actions. Watch your actions; they become habits. Watch your habits; they become character. Watch your character; it becomes your destiny." It's true!

Please understand that changing your life can be a lifelong journey in some areas. Changing your thinking can be immediate, but truly changing your beliefs takes time. If you're in huge debt, it may take you a long time to become debt free. If you are unhealthy, it may take awhile to return to a healthy status. It may take you a long time to repair a broken relationship. It may take you a long time to move your business to the point where it should be.

The fortunate thing about the spiritual area of life is that your position can change instantly. You confess, give your life to God, and let Him take over. That's the beauty about being a believer. That's called salvation. However, *sanctification* is about walking out your salvation. In order to do that, you need to strengthen your relationship with God each day—for the rest of your life. What is your philosophy about your thought life? What do you want your thought life to look like?

You see, you can develop a wholesome philosophy of life and business by embracing new principles to live by. You adopt those principles by changing your beliefs. And you change your beliefs by changing your thinking.

If you read and dissect the previous paragraphs, you have the essence of this book. If I can get you to think about your life and business and develop new beliefs, you will expect a different outcome. When you expect something good to happen, you'll have a better attitude. When you change your attitude, you change your behavior. That's called implementation! And when you change your behavior, you change your performance. When you change your performance, you change your life.

It's up to you to watch your words. Zig Ziglar said a positive attitude won't help you do anything. But it *will* help you do *everything* better than a negative attitude will. When you implement the right things at the right time in the right way, you'll end up with phenomenal performance, which will change your life!

Of course, if it were that simple, this book would not need to be written. The fact is, it's a process. It's a *daily* process.

ACTION STEPS

1. Work on your *Wheel of Life Assessment* at www
   .HowardPartridge.com/success. In order to begin
   the process of setting goals, you need to know where
   you are. This tool helps you assess where you currently are in life.

2. Transfer your results onto the *Wheel of Life* dia-
   gram on page 2 in your *Ziglar Personal Performance
   Planner.*

3. If you are a business owner, complete the *Wheel of
   Business Assessment* as well.

4. Participate in your weekly POD. If you are not in a
   POD yet, go to www.HowardPartridgeInnerCircle
   .com.

Therefore I say to you, all things for which you pray and ask, believe that you have received them, and they will be granted you.
—JESUS (MARK 11:24 NASB)

My son, do not forget my teaching, but keep my commands in your heart, for they will prolong your life many years and bring you peace and prosperity.
—PROVERBS 3:1-2 NIV

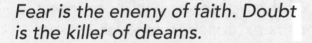

Fear is the enemy of faith. Doubt is the killer of dreams.

You are what you are and where you are because of what has gone into your mind. You can change what you are, and where you are because of what has gone into your mind.
—ZIG ZIGLAR

For God has not given us a spirit of fear, but of power and of love and of a sound mind.
—2 TIMOTHY 1:7 NKJV

A positive attitude won't help you do anything. But it will help you do everything better than a negative attitude will.
—ZIG ZIGLAR

The desire of the righteous will be granted.... the righteous is established forever.
The hope of the righteous brings joy....
The righteous will never be removed...
The mouth of the righteous brings forth wisdom...
—PROVERBS 10:24-25,28,30-31 ESVW

CHAPTER THREE

PRINCIPLE 1: THE POTENTIAL PRINCIPLE

Understanding Your Potential **IMPACTS** Phenomenal Performance

WHO DO YOU THINK YOU ARE?

As I was building my first business, I attended a number of networking groups to improve my skills and build relationships. I was passionate about our industry and wanted to make a difference. One of the groups that met every Monday morning was a group of contractors. This group had a severe case of what Zig Ziglar called *stinkin' thinkin'*. Plus, they had the negative attitude to go with it. They were dressed poorly and some of them hadn't even shaved.

They complained about the industry, about the economy, and bad-mouthed their cheap customers. Each week I confidently strolled through the door with a positive attitude wearing a suit jacket and tie, carrying a briefcase. They laughed at me and said, "Who do you think you are, *Zig Ziglar* or somebody?" The funny thing is, I didn't even know Zig Ziglar at the time. I wouldn't meet him in person for another five years.

But that mocking question ended up being the most important thing I ever learned from Mr. Ziglar. He taught me that man is designed for accomplishment, engineered for success, and endowed with the seeds of greatness. Be honest...did you get up this morning and look in the mirror and say that to yourself? Probably not. But maybe you should have.

Zig also said, "You were born to win." In other words, you were *created* to win in *every* area of life. You were not born to lose. You *are* a phenomenal product, created to *be* phenomenal and to have a phenomenal life, career, and business.

That doesn't mean that you don't need God in your life, and it doesn't mean that you won't have difficulties. It means that you'll be able to perform better in life once you finally understand your powerful God-given potential.

Mr. Ziglar often said, "You cannot *consistently* perform in a manner which is *inconsistent* with the way you see yourself." In other words, if you see yourself as a winner, you will perform like a winner. Remember, humans *do* what humans *see* in their minds.

But that's not the entire picture. As mentioned in the previous chapter, Zig also said, "In order to *be* the winner you were born to be, you must *plan* to win and *prepare* to win before you can *expect* to win. But when you plan to win and prepare to win, you can expect to win."

Zig taught us that all humans suffer from a poor self-image from one degree or another. And because of that, we do not perform at the level that is possible for us. When we come to grips with who we really are and the true potential we have, that belief will dramatically impact our personal lives.

When we understand our true identity and develop a positive self-image, we can begin to believe in the possibilities instead of just seeing the problems. The reason we don't believe we can reach our dreams and goals is because we don't believe we *are* a phenomenal product.

When you accept that God created you for a reason, that He created you to *be* phenomenal, to *do* phenomenal things, and to *have* a phenomenal life, you begin to change the picture of your preferred future. You are now free to dream. So, the most important thing to believe in is the potential you have.

You have phenomenal potential because God has given you a gift. He has given you specific talents and experiences. Your gifts and talents are key to realizing your potential.

People don't implement because deep down they fear they are not good enough or that what they do won't make a difference in the world. They don't believe that what they do has meaning. Or they don't know why they are here, and it skews the reason for living.

Your life matters because God has a plan for your life. You were created for a purpose. We will cover that in The Purpose Principle.

Do you believe that you are born to win? Do you believe that you were designed for accomplishment? Engineered for success? Endowed with the seeds of greatness? Do you believe that you are a phenomenal product, created to be phenomenal, to do phenomenal things, and to have a phenomenal life?

If not, let me ask you a few questions:

- Were you born to lose?

- Were you born to be broke and in debt?

- Were you born to be unhealthy when you could be healthy?

- Are you supposed to have a distant relationship with your Creator?

- Were you created to have difficult relationships with others?

- Are you supposed to be stuck in a job you hate while doing work that has no meaning?

In other words, what areas were you born to be *unsuccessful* in?

The answer is NONE!

To drive this point home, I like to ask my live audiences which one of these areas of life they are supposed to be *unsuccessful*: Spiritual? Mental? Physical? Family? Career? Financial? Personal?

They always respond, "None of them."

Then I ask, "On a scale of 1 to 10, how successful are you supposed to be in each area?"

"Ten!" they exclaim.

To which I add, "Borderline 11." When you realize your phenomenal, God-given potential and live according to the purpose He created you for, you'll be living a *phenomenal* off-the-charts life!

If you could rate yourself a 10 on a scale of 1 to 10 on each area of life, would you be living a dream life? Everyone I've ever asked that question has said, "Yes," except one person. I was on a consulting project for an engineering firm and asked one of the employees that question. The answer she shot back, "I wouldn't want that because then I would have nowhere to go!"

I then explained to her that we develop new dreams and goals for ourselves and we are always growing. When you get to a 10, you'll reach for a bigger, more meaningful goal. It doesn't mean you stop! Go as far as you can, and then you'll see farther. If unbelief keeps us from being a 10 on a scale of 1 to 10, we must identify those beliefs and face reality.

Does that mean you need to be a multimillionaire? Maybe, maybe not. How much money does your vision require? I recently watched a Netflix series titled *Inside Bill's Brain*. It covers some of the problems of the world that Bill Gates and his wife, Melinda, have tried to solve over the years, like the sanitation problem that causes polio. Their work created a stand-alone waste processing plant that is powered by poop and produces clean drinking water. Do you think that cost a *lot* of money? Yes!

Some people need a lot of money because they have a lot they need to do. The Billy Graham ministry, for example, needs a lot of money to do what they do in reaching out world-wide with the gospel.

Does this mean that you are supposed to be the most wealthy or the most physically fit person you know? No, it just means that we weren't born to be unhealthy. In my first book, *7 Secrets of a Phenomenal L.I.F.E.,* I talked about my friend Ray Davis, who was racked with Multiple Sclerosis (MS), a disease that kept him bedridden for many years before he passed away. Even though Ray was in that condition, I would give him a 10 on health because he did everything he could to combat the raging attack on his body.

You can't change anyone, but changing how you approach others opens the door for them to change. You rate your performance based on what you do, not the outcome. You rate yourself on your attitude and effort. Leave the results to God.

Of course you will have trouble. You will have difficulties in this life. Jesus was perfect, yet He was beaten, spat on, and ultimately killed in the most painful, gruesome way possible. But He accomplished His mission because He knew who He was and what His purpose was.

Did you complete your Wheel of Life in the previous chapter Action Steps? If not, go to www.howardpartridge.com/success and do it now.

PROACTIVE

The seductive power of today's media has done a subtle but powerful job in keeping us from becoming the people we really want to become. Directed by some greedy corporations and supported through endless distractions of entertainment, Wisdom and her benefits seem to be lost on us. People adamantly believe things they wouldn't ordinarily believe because they have never investigated what the actual truth is. For example, evolution is widely accepted as truth. No wonder people act like animals!

In the *Ziglar Legacy Training,* we talk about the study of the processionary caterpillar that was performed by a French naturalist. These caterpillars follow the caterpillar in front of them. The caterpillars were placed on the rim of a garden pot and they began to circle the pot. The technician then placed their favorite food in the middle of the pot. But none of the caterpillars broke rank. They continued to follow one another until... they all died. Isn't that how society seems to be? The blind follows the blind, and they all fall in the ditch!

This past year I became a grandfather for the first time. Because I now understand how the mind is molded over a lifetime like the proverbial "boiling of the frog," I am very proactive and intentional about what goes into my granddaughter Gigi's mind. In fact, I dedicated this book to her. When I have the opportunity to be with Gigi, I drop everything I'm doing to hold her and talk to her. She has become my number one priority, because I know that investing in her now will have a big payoff for her in the future.

I want to make sure my granddaughter develops a positive self-image, that she understands her value. I want her to know that God has a plan and a purpose for her life. I want her to understand the possibilities that are available to her. Incidentally, according to Zig Ziglar, a poor self-image is caused by the absence of unconditional love. My intention is to love Gigi unconditionally and to help her understand that God loves her unconditionally.

Obviously, every human being has to think for themselves. At some point Gigi will make her own decisions, but I want her to be equipped to make wise decisions. I don't want her to be a product of our culture, as so many are today. Our culture is dictated and formed by the entertainment industry that does not care about the welfare of our society. The lust for fame and fortune is disguised as what they call "art." Strangers on a screen, who care only about their agenda are raising our kids.

Of course, we have to live in this culture, so we can't avoid it—but our children are exposed to things they are not emotionally equipped to handle. No wonder child suicides are up *100 percent* in the last decade. No wonder there is so much fear and anxiety among our young people. We must set good examples in our homes of what is right and wrong—evil and good.

One of the Scriptures I love is, "Don't be conformed to this world, but be transformed by the renewing of your mind" (Romans 12:2). When we change our thinking about who we are, we change our beliefs, which in turn changes our life for the better.

One of the major stress points in our performance-based, media-driven culture is the affliction of the *comparison disease*. The focus on outward appearances creates a massive internal self-image problem. I came across an image on social media that is a drawing of a woman's face. Written outside the face were the words LOSER, FAILURE, WEAK, but inside the image were the words FREE, FORGIVEN, CHILD OF GOD.

And what about the boys? If you aren't a "bad boy," you just aren't cool. The stress to be the cool cat and to support the culture of drugs, drinking, and sexual immorality is killing our boys too. An interesting fact is that the constant barrage of stress induced by our culture causes a lack of empathy. The poor self-image of troubled young men combined with a life lived deep in the dark digital world produces a deadly cocktail that many times ends up in a drug overdose, suicide, or maybe even a mass shooting.

The comparison disease is the thief of joy. How many girls today think they're ugly because of the beautiful but false images they constantly see on television, movies, magazine, and social media? How many feel unlovable because they don't look as pretty as the images they see on their social media feed? How many feel useless because they don't live the lifestyle of the rich and famous? And what's the outcome of thinking they're no good? Fear, doubt, and an overwhelming amount of stress and anxiety.

Joy and fulfillment come from how you respond to your circumstances, not because of your circumstances. Yes, you want to perform, but you want to perform in the areas that matter and will help you have a truly successful life. Comparing your circumstances or status to someone else's is a certain recipe for a disastrous self-image.

You may have seen a popular video from a stress study using monkeys as the subjects. The monkeys were trained to give the trainer a rock from inside their cage in exchange for a piece of cucumber which they really love. Two monkey cages were placed side by side where the monkeys could see what was happening "next door." The trainer exchanged the cucumber treat for the rock, taking turns between the two monkeys.

Then, the trainer introduced red grapes to one of the monkeys. Red grapes are much more preferred over cucumber by these monkeys. The problem was, he only gave one of the monkeys the grapes as the reward. The monkey that didn't get the grapes threw a fit! When the trainer gave him a cucumber (which he was perfectly happy with just a minute earlier), he threw it back in disgust. It created a great deal of stress in the monkey's mind.

In some ways, we can be like that monkey. In fact, we need a certain amount of stress to keep us safe, but we tend to compare what we get to what others get. We must understand that we don't automatically get what others get. We should be clear on what we want. The good news is that unlike animals, humans have a mind that can create opportunities. If you want grapes instead of cucumbers, you can have grapes!

There are many other ways we are kind of like monkeys. I talked a lot about fear earlier, which causes stress. We are designed with a certain amount of fear to keep us safe, but we were not designed to live with the constant pressure and stress that our modern world serves up. Humans were uniquely created with a mind, and in the image of God. We can have peace when we know God our Creator, and we do not have to live in fear every day. We can choose to live in freedom every day.

Our culture delivers a constant barrage of situations that cause fear and anxiety. If we are going to overcome fear and live by faith so we can be the most positive version of ourselves possible, we must be proactive in our fight against the negative forces. Scripture tells us that "we do not wrestle against flesh and blood, but against the rulers, against the authorities, against the cosmic powers over this present darkness, against the spiritual forces of evil in the heavenly places" (Ephesians 6:12). We have to be focused, diligent, and proactive to win the fight. The battle is within!

Guilt and pride are the two ditches of destruction we tend to fall into. Guilt says we aren't good enough. Pride says we're better than everyone else. Guilt produces an outlook that "Nothing good can happen because I'm no good." Pride produces an attitude that says, "Nobody is the boss of me" and "I'm better than other people." Both guilt and pride are results of a false self-image, and both come from a place of fear.

It's unfortunate that our youth today are getting the idea that the only ways to be successful are to be an entertainer, an athlete, or to win the lottery. We live in a society that is so driven by destructive emotions that wisdom is actually mocked. We need truth. We need wisdom. If we don't capture the truth in our own mind, we'll be victims of reckless emotion.

All of us have challenges and difficulties in this life. You may have health issues, family issues, or financial issues, but the fact remains that you can still have a phenomenal life. You have the potential for greatness, and you have *all* of the qualities of success already within you.

In my own life, most of the difficulties I've had were brought on by something I did to myself. I suffered financially because of bad decisions. I suffered healthwise because I didn't eat right and exercise. When I have difficulties with my wife, it's usually because I did something wrong.

We have all seen people overcome extreme difficulties in life, and we should judge ourselves based on what we do about our circumstances, not on the circumstances themselves. We are all born into a fallen world, surrounded by obstacles to overcome. Regardless of your circumstances, you are still a phenomenal product, created to be phenomenal, to do phenomenal things, and to have a phenomenal life.

What does all of this have to do with implementation? Everything! Deep down, we all want the same things in life—love, food and water, shelter, and to feel safe—but when our actions don't support our goal, we begin to think that something is wrong with us. We have to understand that just like there is a God, there is also an enemy. That does not mean we can blame the devil, just like we can't *blame* God.

The battle is in our mind and *for* our mind. The enemy attacks us through our *identity.* If you look at what's happening in our culture today, whether political, religious, or social, it's all about identity. We all want to express our identity. The question is, "Will the identity you have assumed help you reach the goals you really want in life?"

We all need to know that we are fearfully and wonderfully made. You are made in *God's* image. And if you have accepted God's proposal to know Him through His Son Jesus Christ, His Holy Spirit is *inside* you!

In the last chapter of my book *Think and Be Phenomenal,* I share seventy-three Scriptures that reveal your true identity in Christ as a believer. Most Christians don't even know who they are in Christ. What you need to know is that you are a *child* of the Most High God!

But that is not what our culture teaches us. Recently I saw a Geico commercial that opens with this question: "Did you know Pinocchio was a bad motivational speaker?" As the speaker looked around the room, he continued, "I look around this room and I see nothing but untapped potential." His nose got longer and longer as he pointed to each person and told them they have potential. The ad was meant to be funny, but how many people take that sneer personally and believe they have no potential, no value?

You absolutely *do* have potential! If you didn't, God would not have put you here! Have you heard of Nick Vujicic? Nick was born with no arms and no legs. He was mocked as a kid and he considered committing suicide; but today, he's a respected worldwide speaker and author. He travels the world inspiring kids to get the right picture of themselves. Nick may not have arms and legs, but he knows who he is inside! And he knows *Whose* he is.

All of us have different goals and differing circumstances. What we *do* with those circumstances is the key. Don't live your life by circumstance. Live your life by vision. And the most important vision you can have is *who* you are.

Humans have always searched for significance through identity. Every human being wants to feel important, but we tend to go about it in all the wrong ways. We strive for power through accumulating wealth or fame. Or, we rebel to get attention from others so we can feel significant.

The longing for significance is built inside us because we *are* significant! I often ask people how they are doing. If they say anything less than "phenomenal," I remind them they are phenomenal. Why? Because God made them! And everything He makes is phenomenal, right?

We all long for significance. It's ingrained in us. But like most things, since we live in a fallen world and we are naturally driven by fleshly desires, we seek significance by creating a false identity.

God created you for a reason. He has given you specific gifts. Each one of us has a unique fingerprint. Be grateful for who God made you to be, and understand that life is about becoming *that* person. Scripture teaches us to be content with food and covering, but it also teaches us to grow spiritually and to be wise. Be content with what you have, but never be satisfied with who you are becoming—as you continue to discover your phenomenal potential. The amazing thing about life is that it's a journey of discovering who we already are!

Zig Ziglar often said, "Out of all the attitudes we can acquire, surely the attitude of gratitude is the most important and by far the most life changing." Why is that? Because when we are grateful, our focus is on God and others—not on ourselves.

A positive self-image is key. Remember, you cannot consistently *perform* in a manner that is *inconsistent* with how you see yourself. So, who do you think you are? Do you *believe* that you are designed for accomplishment? Do you *believe* you are engineered for success? Do you *believe* you are endowed with the seeds of greatness? Do you *believe* that God doesn't make junk? Do you *believe* you are born to win? Do you *believe* you are a phenomenal product? Don't think too highly of yourself, but don't think too small of yourself either.

Who do *you* believe you are? *Whose* do you believe you are? Your belief is going to determine what you do and don't do—even if you are not aware of the belief. We do what we value, and we value what we do. If you want to come to grips with what you truly believe, just watch your actions. Look at how you use money. Look at how you take care of yourself and others. Look at how you relate to God. Look at how you approach life.

Here are a few questions for you:

- Is your chosen identity getting you where you want to go?

- Is it creating joy and fulfillment in your life?

- What do *you* choose to put into *your* mind?

- What is your confession?

- What's your affirmation?

- Who do you want to become?

PERSONALITY

Everyone has a gift. You are a unique creation. You have been given unique abilities. You have been made special. You also have skills, abilities, and knowledge no one else has. You have value. That's why the Geico commercial makes me so angry—because *everyone* has *value* and *potential*.

God highly values each of us, and He gave each one of us a gift we should value. My training and coaching company, Phenomenal Products, was named by my fifteen-year-old nephew, who at the time had worn out every other family member's welcome and was sleeping on my couch. We were brainstorming names for this new venture, and the when the word *phenomenal* popped out of his mouth, I *knew* it was the winner. His contribution was of value, and I appreciated him for his creativity.

One of your gifts is your personality style. You can use that gift to help yourself or to hurt yourself. You can use it to help your cause or hurt your cause. You can use it to help others or hurt others. Some people are outgoing, and some are reserved. Some are more task oriented, and some are more people-oriented. I have found that understanding your unique personality style is extremely important.

Understanding yourself and how you are uniquely wired helps you to make better choices for your career, to understand your strengths and weaknesses, and to build stronger relationships with others.

Your personality style will also have a dramatic effect on how you implement. For example, a high D personality will get a boatload of stuff done, but may leave destruction in the wake. A high I may influence lots of people, but may have lost his or her daily planner. A high S may serve a great deal of people, but fail to implement the things that will help them succeed personally. A high C will plan thoroughly, but may procrastinate longer than necessary.

Understanding your personality style is vital to understanding your performance. Discover your unique personality style at www.HowardPartridge.com/disc.

PRESENTS

In closing this chapter, let me share another story I learned from Zig. It's a story about a man in southeast Texas during the depression. Times were tough and he was desperate for money, so he put his land up for sale. An oilman stopped by one day and told the man the oil company had reason to believe there was oil on his property. And if he would allow them to dig for it, they would share the profits.

Well, the man had nothing to lose and everything to gain, so he agreed. Back then the oil derricks were made of wood and the bigger the gusher, the greater the destruction. They struck oil and the derrick was obliterated. A hundred thousand gallons spewed out before they could get it capped. It became the largest producing oil well in history at that time, and the man who owned the land became an instant millionaire.

Or did he?

You see, he was already a millionaire. The oil was already there. It just needed to be discovered and brought to the surface so it could be taken to market. The same is true about your potential and your gift. It's already there. It's inside you. It just needs to be discovered and brought to the surface, so it can be taken to the marketplace. Your talent, your skill, and your personality are needed in our world. Your potential is there. It's just untapped and undeveloped.

Don't let unbelief keep you from developing and using your gift. When you understand your *present* potential, you'll see the phenomenal power that is in your future. When you know who you are and Whose you are, you'll have peace that you're on the right track. So, don't be conformed to the world, but be transformed by the renewing of your mind. Allow God to transform you into the person you are supposed to be.

Discover your gift, dig it up, develop it, and deliver it to the world.

ACTION STEPS

1. Read pages 3-5 in your *Ziglar Personal Performance Planner.* In this section, you learn the Goal Reaching Process. Reflect on your *Wheel of Life* and be thinking about areas you would like to change.

2. Participate in your weekly POD.

Man is designed for accomplishment, engineered for success and endowed with the seeds of greatness.

—ZIG ZIGLAR

You are a phenomenal product, created to be phenomenal, to do phenomenal things and to have a phenomenal life.

—HOWARD PARTRIDGE

You cannot consistently perform in a manner that is inconsistent with the way you see yourself.

—ZIG ZIGLAR

When you know who you are, and whose you are, you'll have peace in your heart.

—HOWARD PARTRIDGE

Do not be conformed to this world, but be transformed by the renewal of your mind, that by testing you may discern what is the will of God, what is good and acceptable and perfect.

—ROMANS 12:2 ESV

CHAPTER FOUR

PRINCIPLE 2: THE PICTURE PRINCIPLE

A Compelling Picture **IMAGINES** Phenomenal Performance

WHAT DO YOU SEE?

I wrote a book titled *Discover Your Phenomenal Dream Life* in which I shared seven ways to dream. The simplest one is just to imagine that you could rate your life a 10 on a scale of 1 to 10 on the Wheel of Life, mentioned in the previous chapter.

One of the stories I share in my "dream book" is about my dream of owning a specific piece of property and building a dream house next to my favorite beach near Destin, Florida. It was a big dream for me, and I encountered many obstacles along the way.

Shortly after we moved in, a visitor asked me how long we had lived there. "Twenty years," I responded. "I thought you just moved in!" the visitor exclaimed, obviously confused. I shared that I had been living there in my *mind* since 1997, when I first bought the property.

Once I had the *picture* fixed in my mind, I didn't let it escape. For years, a movie was playing in my mind of Denise and I living there. This has been a lifelong dream actually. I grew up on welfare in Mobile, Alabama, and always loved going to the beach. When I found Destin, it became my obsession to own something, anything there. I had a picture of the Seaside Post Office in my office that I looked at every day. I imagined Denise and I riding bikes through Seaside.

Eventually, we bought a little one-room efficiency condo. It was just *one* room! The tiny kitchen was in the same room, a sofa, and a small table where only two people could sit at a time. The *only* door in the entire unit was a bathroom door. But it was enough. It was a sixty-second walk to the beach.

One evening, we were riding our bikes around Seaside, passing the cute little post office, and I realized my vision from the poster had come true. Then, the next piece of the picture came together as we built our beautiful home next to my favorite beach. We not only have an amazing second home, but it was a great investment as well. The moment the house was completed, it was worth more than what I spent to build it. That's what I call *better than phenomenal!*

As I share in my "dream book," this is an example of a personal dream. My personal dream may not mean anything to you, but when people come to visit, they are inspired to dream bigger. But there's bigger picture for all of us. It's what business author Michael Gerber calls the *"impersonal* dream" in his phenomenal book, *Awaken the Entrepreneur Within.*

The impersonal dream is the dream that will change the world. It's the one that will make a difference in the lives of others. This picture will come directly from your *purpose.* If your purpose is to solve the world hunger problem, and your passionate about feeding people, then your impersonal dream will most likely be related to that.

My impersonal dream is for every person in the world to discover and live out their purpose. My dream is that every person on the planet would understand who they are and why they are here—to have a meaningful life and meaningful work.

Every sports team has the same vision: to ultimately win the championship. But there are many goals along the way. Implement the play that is in front of you consistently and you'll eventually score and keep the other team from scoring and you win the game. Win enough games, and you win the championship.

Before I started writing this book, I taught these principles to my Inner Circle Coaching Members. The NBA Finals were in progress at the time, and I easily predicted who would win. In fact, I can predict who will win every game every time—without Biff's *Sports Almanac* from the movie *Back to the Future.* How did I know? Because I knew that the team that *performed* the best would win!

Sometimes a bad call costs someone a game, but that's how life can be. Just because you get a bad call once in a while doesn't mean you can make excuses for not being successful.

You can make excuses or you can choose to consistently perform. When you consistently perform, you will consistently win. You can have results or you can have excuses, but you can't have both.

Speaking of winning consistently, what is it about humans that we cannot stand the person or team that consistently wins? Don't you want to consistently win? What if people hated you because *you* were a consistent winner? We live in a fast-paced performance-based society. We seem to judge everything by performance. Even our identity.

To be clear, this book is not about keeping up with others or about stressing yourself out to reach bigger and bigger goals just for show or to enhance your identity or status. It's about implementing the things that are important to you based on *your* purpose in life. We all have different goals, and we should celebrate the success of others, rather than envy their accomplishments.

And remember, as we talked about the comparison disease in the previous chapter, we shouldn't judge ourselves based on what others accomplish, and we shouldn't be jealous of what others have. This creates a great deal of stress;when you are stressed, you will not perform at your highest level.

Obviously, if you are in a specific competition, you should perform at your highest level. But in life and business, you are competing with your own goal. You are competing with your own performance. Of course, you have competition in business, but when you become obsessed with the competition, that deadly fear kicks in again, and you give up your peace and joy.

Do you have a compelling vision for your life or for your business? Do you have a dream? Can you *see* where you want to go? Remember the secret ingredient of success is *desire*. If you don't really *want* something, you won't do the things you need to do to make it happen. Desire comes from a *vision*.

Most people can identify the problems they have, but they have trouble with the vision part. The dream for many is to just get through the day. I don't think that's what God had in mind when He created you. People don't allow themselves to dream bigger. Fear gets in the way of faith. They don't believe. Remember the underlying reason for FTI is a lack of *belief*. When you believe in your potential, have a strong purpose pulling you, and you have the right people around you, you're set up to dream bigger and to think bigger.

The bigger the dream, the more that is required of you. The bigger the dream, the stronger the team needs to be. If you knew you could accomplish *anything*, what would it be? If you allowed yourself to simply dream for a moment, and you knew you couldn't fail, what would you want to accomplish in your life?

- What would you do?
- What would your lifestyle be?
- What would your financial position be?
- What would your health look like?
- What would you learn?
- Where would you travel?
- What would you own?

- Who would you spend time with?
- What would your family life look like?
- What would you think about?
- What would your spiritual life look like?

If you took a moment to simply *dream* and you *believed* anything was possible, what would that look like?

Remember that your beliefs are deeply ingrained and that many of them are hidden. A couple of years ago, I was studying some material and the question, "Could you be a billionaire?" came up. What would *your* response be to that question?

My mental response was, *Of course I can!* But, that's the easy question. The better question is, *"Should* I be a billionaire?" Do I *need* to be a billionaire? If yes, *why?*

Speaking of money, have you ever thought about how much money you are supposed to have? How much you are supposed to make? Well, here's the answer...you should have the amount of money you are *supposed* to have. You should have the amount of money you are *supposed* to make to reach your vision. Simple, right? Well, that means you have to have a vision for your life and for your business or career.

Humans do what humans see. That's why you *need* a dream. You *need* a vision. A phenomenal picture imagines phenomenal performance. A compelling picture engages your imagination. My dream book will help you unlock your imagination. And my book *Think and Be Phenomenal* will help you unlock your thinking. Remember, when you change your thinking, you change your beliefs. When you change your beliefs, you change your expectations.

Vision is about seeing the picture. Faith is about expecting the vision to come true. Zig says, "You have to *see* the reaching in your *mind* before actually arriving at the destination." As I write this piece, I'm on the front porch of an Italian Villa in the middle of Tuscany, Italy. *Tenuti di Spannochia* is a self-sustainable farm that grows enough organic food and raises enough animals to feed the staff, a gaggle of interns, and the various groups that stay there. Of course, a meal is not complete without wine in Italy, so they make their own wine too!

The icon of the property is a 12th-century Tuscan castle, surrounded by vineyards, organic gardens, and breathtaking views of rich green rolling hills. As I look up from my computer and peer through the ancient sun-drenched plastered arches, I see the college students busily working early in the morning. They are interning in the areas of winemaking, cooking, and caring for livestock. Obviously they are pursuing a career, but I sense that many of them are living out their purpose and bringing their gifts to the world to make a difference. They have a vision of a less wasteful, more sustainable world.

An inspirational place like this is the perfect setting to write; therefore, perhaps like the interns, I'm fulfilling my personal vision, as well as my impersonal vision. My nephew organizes a trip to Tuscany every year, and this is our third trip with his group. He brought his twelve-year-old daughter with him this time and she's really passionate about animals, especially pigs!

The farm raises pigs to make prosciutto, so we took a walk to see them. She was so excited about the little piglets. As we made our way back down the dirt road, she began to rattle off her dream about having lots of animals. She wants to have pigs live in her house with her when she grows up. I asked her what she would do about the pigs pooping in the house and she told me she had already thought about that and she would train them to "take care of their business" on a tray that would catapult out the window.

Now, I don't know much about pigs and maybe they can be house-trained, but as she shared her idea about the catapult, the look on her mom's face, eyebrows raised, told me that her daughter has lots of ideas. Some may or may not be realistic. But we can learn something from people like Mae. We should all dream like a twelve-year-old. We should have the mind of a child when we dream, because the fact is that unrealistic dreams can lead to ideas that are truly phenomenal. Author and small business guru Michael E. Gerber shares that when dreaming, "We start with a blank piece of paper and a beginner's mind."

The idea of Phenomenal Products was born on a long, dark stretch of Texas highway late one night as a former employee and I were brainstorming, drinking a soda, and chewing on beef jerky. We dreamed about ways to help business owners. The original idea was so unrealistic and so crazy I won't even mention it here, but it is truly amazing what has happened as a result of freely thinking without any limitations. That crazy brainstorming session turned into a coaching program that is helping people around the world. Unrealistic ideas turn into a realistic vision.

You never can tell exactly what your vision is going to look like or feel like in the end, but you have to start somewhere. Simply getting a picture that you are passionate about and keeping in mind that you have the potential to pull it off, begins to unlock the possibilities for your life and for your business.

PAYMENT

It's vitally important to have the right vision, because someone will have to pay for it. Many times, people have a passion for something that may be destructive to them, or it doesn't pass the "Is it fair to everyone involved?" test. When the Ziglar team first came up with the tagline "Inspiring True Performance," the definition was "True performance is the progression of an ideal goal or accomplishment." When Zig looked at it, he added four words: "that benefits everyone involved."

You cannot expect others to pay for your dream. You must pay for your own dream. Many times the cost is just too much for the benefit. As my friend Ellen Rohr likes to say, "The juice ain't worth the squeeze." A worthy goal is one that doesn't cost you, your family, your faith, or your health. A worthy goal and even a dream requires prudence to make sure you are making wise choices instead of foolish ones.

Think big, but act wise. Dream big, but act small. Think outrageous, but act with love, kindness, and humility. Faith doesn't have to be some crazy, outlandish, throw caution to the wind affair. Reaching a worthy goal is hard enough! Reaching a big dream that will truly change the world, not just make you feel good, is hard enough without adding the burden of foolishness.

PRIDE

Two decades of coaching have taught me that people can heavily pursue an idea that doesn't have a lot of merit. The driving force is *pride*. They don't want to admit they are wrong. Just watch the television *Shark Tank*. Occasionally, you have someone come along with a really bad idea. They aren't making any money, and they are ruining their lives for the idea. After *all* the experts tell them it's a bad idea, they get on camera after the encounter, with tears in their eyes, and defiantly insist they won't give up. If you're traveling in the wrong direction, you need to stop and turn around.

The right kind of pride can be a good thing. You should take pride in your work, for example. You should take pride in how you dress. You should take pride in your home. The negative type of pride is called *vanity*. We should have a healthy self-image, but should not be prideful in that sense.

As we will discuss in The People Principle chapter, successful people get wise advice and thrive from knowledge and understanding. The proverb that Phenomenal Products was founded on is "Without consultation, plans are frustrated, but with many counselors they succeed." We often don't have the information we really need to accomplish a big goal or dream.

Another reason people don't want input from others is because they won't get the credit. This has always baffled me in the coaching space. Someone who is obviously struggling won't take advice from anyone else. They bury their heads in the sand in total obstinance and continue in their pain and misery. One of the most freeing things we can do is *admit* that we need help!

Gary Keller's definition of success is "Getting what you want." But in order to do that you have to know what you want. And as we've already covered, in order to reach big goals, you have to have a big desire and big faith. Clearly identifying your goals is very important. Robert A. Heinlein said, "In the absence of clearly defined goals, we become strangely loyal to performing daily trivia until ultimately we become enslaved by it." I call that FTI.

You may be a person who has been "successful" without writing down goals and going through the goal-setting process, but I can guarantee that you have goals. You have principles you live by which create habit goals. You have goals of being somewhere every day. You have a goal to act a certain way.

It's a rare person who reaches goals naturally. Most people need a goals *program.* Most people need support, encouragement, and accountability to reach their goals. And if you are already an achiever, a goals program will help you.

I'm an implementer. But setting goals according to a proven process has been very helpful to me. I have lots of ideas, so I need a way to capture the ideas and to prioritize my goals. And I need support to reach those goals. And I need people to help me stay focused and accountable. No one succeeds alone.

Goals come in four categories:

1. **BE** Goals. A "BE" goal is a habit goal. You want to *be* a certain kind of person. You want to *be* a phenomenal person of faith, a phenomenal spouse or parent, etc.

2. **DO** Goals. A "DO" goal is something you want to accomplish. Maybe your goal is to write a book. I can tell you from personal experience that writing books is a phenomenal learning process about FTI. Maybe it's your goal to *do* your best to win a competition.

3. **HAVE** Goals. Maybe you would like to *have* a new car, new house, or something tangible. That's a "HAVE" goal.

4. **GIVE** Goals. Giving is the key to true fulfillment. Maybe you want to *give* away a certain amount of money, or you want to *give* time in service to others. This is a noble goal indeed.

Ziglar has a complete, proven goals program, so I will not spend time on how to set goals right now, but your *Ziglar Personal Performance Planner* reveals the exact steps to take. Just follow the directions, and you will reach more of your goals.

ACTION STEPS

1. Fill out page 6 (The Dream List) in Your *Ziglar Personal Performance Planner.*

2. Participate in your weekly POD.

Out of all the attitudes we can acquire, surely the attitude of gratitude is the most important and by far the most life changing.
—ZIG ZIGLAR

One's pride will bring him low, but he who is lowly in spirit will obtain honor.
—PROVERBS 29:23 ESV

Blessed is the one who finds wisdom, the one who gets understanding.
—PROVERBS 3:13 ESV

Be content with what you have. But never be content with your personal growth.
—HOWARD PARTRIDGE

Don't live your life by circumstance. Live your life by vision. And the most important vision you can have is who you are.

—HOWARD PARTRIDGE

A positive attitude won't help you do anything. But it will help you do everything better than a negative attitude will.

—ZIG ZIGLAR

The way of a fool is right in his own eyes, but a wise man listens to advice.

—PROVERBS 12:15 ESV

Whoever works his land will have plenty of bread, but he who follows worthless pursuits lacks sense.

—PROVERBS 12:11 ESV

CHAPTER FIVE

PRINCIPLE 3: THE PURPOSE PRINCIPLE

Knowing Your Purpose **INSPIRES** Phenomenal Performance

WHY DO YOU DO WHAT YOU DO?

Mark Twain quipped, "The two most important days in any person's life is the day they were born and the day they find out why." If you don't know your purpose, you won't have the energy you need to pursue your most meaningful goals.

We should always ask ourselves *why* we do what we do. We should think about our life goals and *why* we want them. We should think about the principles we live by and ask why they matter. In fact, we should continually ask ourselves these questions on a daily basis. Everything we do should have a *why* behind it.

When you know your purpose, you'll be inspired. When you finally realize that God made you for a reason, it gives you an amazing amount of energy and confidence. When your life and your work have a higher calling, you will be more energized to pursue it with a greater level of commitment and passion.

Also, when you don't know your purpose, you'll set the wrong goals. You'll be headed in the wrong direction. As someone aptly said, "The only thing worse than climbing the ladder of success is realizing it is leaning against the wrong wall."

You may not know what your life calling is quite yet. Most people don't. But when you understand the purpose of living—of becoming—and you know that the reason you were born will show up sooner or later, you will live life with more joy and fulfillment.

People sometimes ask me why I write books and present at seminars and coach people. The answer is simple. I do what I do because I am *called* to do it. I didn't always know that. At one point, it was just a business. Yes, I cared about people and their outcome, and my clients were successful as a result, but it didn't have the level of meaning for me, because I forgot that it was something God had birthed. I was thinking about quitting, but when I remembered my purpose and changed my perspective, everything changed.

When I accepted and engaged in the purpose of what I do, I had more inspiration to move forward. The results speak for themselves. Every day we hear stories of people who have changed their lives and businesses through our work. That inspires me to do even more.

Phenomenal Products is not a job, and it's not a business. It's a calling. There was also a time when I wanted to get rid of my first business. Obviously, this is a pattern! It's probably a pattern in every business owner's life, because it's not easy to build a business. Many years ago, I wanted to go into full-time ministry. I even felt a little awkward about making money—that somehow it was dirty, even evil. But God showed me that my business *was* my ministry. And today, that business still makes record sales and profits; more importantly, it helps thirty-three families live *their* dreams.

Some of our employees are the first in their entire family history to own a home. Their kids are the first ones *ever* to attend college. Now, that's making a difference! In our business training, we teach our coaching clients to create their purpose statement. In a business, the purpose statement considers what customers would miss out on if that business didn't exist. When the team members know *why* the business exists, they are more engaged, and their work is more meaningful. It's easy to get caught up in the day-to-day life. We have to remember our purpose.

What would your world miss out on if *you* didn't exist? What will the world miss out on if you don't live out your purpose?

Knowing your purpose—also called your *why,* or your *calling*—is extremely important because as we have already discussed in detail, you were created as a unique human being. The question is why were you created? You've probably heard that God has a plan for your life. Discovering that plan is part of your life journey. You may not know your life calling yet. Many people discover their purpose later in life, but that doesn't mean we can't get some clues now.

Three clues to discover your purpose:

1. **Your potential.** Your gifts, talents, and experiences. Can you see why the chapter on The Potential Principle is so important? You can't discover *why* you are here until you know *who* you are!

2. **The problem.** What is the problem in the world you want to solve? When you think about all of the problems of the world, which one bothers you the most?

3. **Your passion.** What do you love to do? What would you do for free?

When you are passionate about solving a problem that afflicts the world, you'll probably find clues to your purpose. Successful businessman and syndicated radio host Dave Ramsey is passionate about America's debt problems. What does he love to do? Teach. In fact, before he was on the radio, he taught his Financial Peace course in a church Sunday school. Zig Ziglar wanted to solve a self-image problem. What was he passionate about doing? Writing and speaking.

I never really wanted to be a "businessman." I just wanted to serve my customers and make them happy. I just wanted to have a great lifestyle. The image of a *businessman* seemed like a hard-charging, stressed-out, unhappy, greedy person. But then I learned that I could be a successful business person and still be myself! I learned that I can be generous, fun loving, and still be phenomenally successful.

One of the reasons I was contemplating quitting Phenomenal Products is because I was under the impression that I saw others in the coaching space who were intentionally aloof, guru-types who would only let people get near them if they paid higher and higher amounts of money. You had to join the next level to be in their presence. There are many coaches like that. They make money, but I wonder about their level of joy and fulfillment.

By understanding my purpose and learning from people like Zig, who loved being with and genuinely helping people, I began to realize I could still be the joyous, happy, goofy Howard, who loves to laugh and play and be silly and still command the highest prices for coaching.

The problem I want solved in the world is a *belief* problem. I want you to understand that you *can* succeed because you are a phenomenal product! You *can* succeed in business and in life because you were born to win! I also have the gifts, talents, and experience to help others, and I'm passionate about solving the problem. I have crystal clear answers for the three questions about my purpose.

The other day I was sitting on "my" beach. My dream home is perfectly situated next to my favorite beach in the entire world, as mentioned previously. There are three and a half miles of unspoiled white-sand beach, graced by crystal clear emerald green water that mirrors the Caribbean. The fourteen homes in our little cul-de-sac have a special deed that is unusual in the area. We actually own the beach all the way to the waterline.

Recently there was a legal squabble between the home-owners and the locals who want full access to "our" beach. As a result, "Private Beach" signs were posted with instructions to "Walk along the waterline." But now the signs cause people to notice the huge mansions on the beach even more. Our beach house is relatively small and plain compared to our neighbors' homes.

One day I was sitting near the water, on this huge beach all by myself, as two mothers with their two teenage daughters walked by and stopped. "Do you live here?" one asked. "Yes, I do," I politely replied. "Wow, could you give our daughters some tips on making good choices?" she asked.

First off, this lady didn't know me. She assumed I had made good choices because I have a home there, which is true; but she had no idea of my character or my values. I guess I could give myself more credit and assume that she could tell I was a good guy. But what she definitely didn't know about was my passion to help others become successful. She had no idea that she was talking to *Mr. Phenomenal.* Was she ready for the "phenomenal talk," as my friends jokingly call it? And more importantly, were the two teenagers ready for what I was about to tell them?

What do you think I told them? I told them they were phe-nomenal. I told them God made them that way. That He created them for a reason, and that life was about figuring out what that reason was. I didn't tell them to get good grades or get a career. In fact, the lady asked me if I went to college. "Nope. I barely got out of high school," I shot back. I shared that I made poor choices early in life, and that if I had it to do over again, I would have gone to college, but that was beside the point.

I told them the most important thing is to know who you are and why you're here. I think they got more than they bargained for that morning, and probably not what they were expecting! What's the point? The point is that I will pour the "phenomenal talk" out on perfect strangers because I am passionate about solving the problem, and I have the potential to do it!

Another way of saying this can be found in a book by John Maxwell titled *Intentional Living*. The book asks three important questions to help us get clues about our purpose:

1. What do you cry about?
2. What do you sing about?
3. What do you dream about?

I cry about the sea of humanity who don't know why they are here and what to do about it. I cry about business owners who feel like slaves to their business and don't have the freedom they deserve.

What do I sing about; what am I passionate about? I love personal development and small business. I talk about those things whether I get paid or not. Getting paid helps me help more people.

What do I dream about? I dream of a world where people know their calling and are using their gifts to glorify God and reach their full potential. I dream of business owners spending time with their families rather than being slaves to their businesses.

Without a purpose, we become what Zig calls a "wandering generality" rather than a "meaningful specific." Knowing your purpose inspires phenomenal performance because when you realize that you are truly special, and that God has a special mission for you, a fire kindles inside you that no one can extinguish. Once the fire gets lit, there is no stopping it.

When Reverend Billy Graham passed away, I listened to hours of news coverage about his life. When someone famous passes away, an abundance of information is shared about the person's life that would not ordinarily be shared. In one interview, Billy Graham confessed that many times when he left home for a crusade, he would cry as he drove down that long driveway away from his North Carolina mountaintop home, knowing he would not see his family for weeks, maybe months. "But the call of God was so strong on my life, that I had to go," he confessed. From that first crusade in 1947 until today, Billy Graham and his ministries have touched millions of lives worldwide, and his legacy lives on through his massive ministry, Billy Graham Evangelistic Association, and the work of his children and grandchildren.

Zig Ziglar said, "You'll find your purpose where deep passion meets the world's need." Another way to say that is, "You'll find your purpose where deep passion meets the world's problem." There are plenty of problems in the world. Pick one you are passionate about!

Many small business owners feel like slaves to their businesses, but that's not their biggest problem. The biggest problem is being so overwhelmed with the things they need to do, they don't have a life outside of their businesses. They don't have freedom. So my purpose is *to help them have more life. To live in freedom every day.*

We should all work hard. In fact, when you find your purpose, you'll probably work even harder, but your work will be more meaningful to you. It's more meaningful work because you understand the why behind it. You understand *why* you're doing it, not just to make money and not just to pay the bills.

Zig Ziglar also said that "Planes are built for flying. Ships were built for sailing. Houses were built for living, and man was built for a purpose." Think about this. What happens to a plane if doesn't fly? It falls apart. What happens to a ship if it just sits in the harbor? Barnacles and corrosion attach to it and it falls apart. What happens to a house if it sits empty and nobody lives in it? It falls apart. What happens to people when they don't live on purpose? They fall apart.

We don't experience the joy and fulfillment of life we are searching for when we don't know our purpose. As John Maxwell has said, "When there's hope for the future, there's power in the present." Knowing your purpose gives you hope. When you have hope, you know there's a future. You know that circumstances can change and that gives you power right now.

- What do *you* cry about?
- What problem do *you* want solved?
- What do *you* sing, talk about?
- What would *you* do for free?

- What do *you* dream about?

PRAYER

Prayer plays a very important role in living out the principles of phenomenal performance. Because God created you as a unique individual and has a specific, unique purpose for you, don't you think He wants you to know what it is? A loving God wouldn't create you and just desert you.

God may not let you in on all the details yet, but He desperately wants to spend time with you. Just like humans want their children to share their hearts, your heavenly Father wants to hear from you, and you certainly want to hear from Him! Ask God what His plan and His purpose is for your life. What burden has He put on your heart? What gifts has He given you? Who are the people He has put in your life?

A few months ago, I felt that God wanted to share something with me. I felt there was something I was supposed to be doing, but I couldn't put my finger on it. I decided to take four days off and do a digital fast at my beach home in Florida. No social media, no email, no texting, with the exception for my wife and my assistant, and even then I shared with the two of them that I would only check text messages in the morning and in the evening. And I spoke to my wife over the phone each day.

I didn't work on any projects at all. No work whatsoever. I walked the beach every day and I prayed throughout the day, asking God what was going on. After the second day, I felt led to go into my closet and pull out my *Ziglar Personal*

Performance Planner from 2012. I do a mini-journal every week in my planner that records the highs and lows of the week. It's a phenomenal exercise to go back to previous years to see what I was thinking about and working on. As I flipped through the pages, a journal entry jumped off the page about a vision I had of helping our youth learn the philosophies I am sharing in this book.

I spent the remaining two days praying through the idea that God reminded me of, and I remembered how my *Destin Dream Retreat* had such an impact on a few of the kids who had attended with their parents, specifically Samuel and Daniel Campos, who were only seven and eight years old at the time.

They joyfully received the "phenomenal" message. After returning to school after summer break, they both shared the phenomenal message with their classmates. Both of them became class president of their grade that year!

Before this four-day prayer session, I was considering not even holding that event because it's hard for some of our members to travel that far, it's expensive to stay in Destin during the summer, and not everyone is a beach lover like me.

When I told Carlos Campos, the boys' father, that I was thinking about not holding the next year, he shot back, "You better do it! My boys are going to be *extremely* disappointed!" I couldn't disappoint the two boys who were spreading "phenomenal" all over their school, and now I was equipped with a Word from God. I decided to encourage our Inner Circle Members to bring their kids to the next retreat, and I promised to have some youth training for them.

It just so happened that not too long before that, Alexandra Ziglar and I were talking about Zig Ziglar's I CAN course that was in hundreds of grade schools in the 1990s. I borrowed the huge manual from Laurie Magers, Zig's long-time executive assistant, dusted it off, and started going through it. After choosing some content from the I CAN course for the younger ones and some material from our *Ziglar Youth Training*, I was all set.

Ninety people attended the retreat, and almost half were kids—and they absolutely loved it! But more importantly, those young ones left the beach knowing their value and having a great hope for the future. Even the teenagers! The parents were so impressed that they are now asking me when our next youth training would be held. Then, God came through again. He brought people across my path who can help me make Phenomenal Youth a reality.

The point of this story is that God has a purpose for your life and work, but you may not be able to hear Him without taking some time to earnestly pray.

PATH

God will also help you find your unique path. When you find your *why* you'll find your *way*. When you find your *purpose,* you'll find the *path* to walk out your purpose. Many people are trying to find their way in life. They are trying to find their path. They are trying to find their groove. My contention is that when you begin to discover your unique purpose, you'll find your unique path.

The path you find may not be the *permanent* path. It rarely is. But in order to find your ultimate road to a meaningful life, you have to get on the road. You need to get on *a* path to get where you want to go. Begin to test a few roads to find the best one for you. One road leads to another, and that road leads to another.

I believe and have experienced that you'll find your purpose in God's timing. But just sitting still isn't going to work. God won't do it without you, and you *can't* do it without Him. Worse is being on the wrong road. Many times, humans rebel against their calling and run as fast as they can down the wrong road for all the wrong reasons.

Some of the questions to ask yourself:

- Does my purpose serve the world in a positive way, or does it exist to serve me alone?
- Is my purpose fair to everyone involved?
- Am I forcing others to sacrifice for my purpose?
- Does my purpose promote spiritual, mental, and physical health?

PURPOSE EXERCISE

I encourage you to complete this exercise honestly and candidly. You may discover your purpose or at least move closer to finding the right path to begin your journey.

My potential: What are my gifts?

_____

_____

_____

_____

_____

_____

_____

My problem: What do I want to see solved in the world?

_____

_____

_____

_____

_____

_____

My passion: What do I talk about?

_____

_____

_____

_____

_____

_____

_____

My purpose: What am I called to? Which leads to me to what path?

_____

_____

_____

_____

_____

My path: What do I dream about?

_____

_____

_____

_____

_____

ACTION STEPS

1. Complete the Purpose Exercise.

2. Fill out page 7 in Your *Ziglar Personal Performance Planner.* This is where you list your biggest goals and describe *why* they are important to you!

3. Participate in your weekly POD.

The two most important days in any person's life is the day they were born and the day they find out why.

—MARK TWAIN

You'll find your purpose where deep passion meets the world's need.

—ZIG ZIGLAR

Planes are built for flying. Ships were built for sailing. Houses were built for living, and man was built for a purpose.

—ZIG ZIGLAR

Many are the plans in the mind of a man, but it is the purpose of the Lord that will stand.

—PROVERBS 19:21 ESV

When you find your why, you'll find your way.

—UNKNOWN

When there is hope for the future, there is power in the present.

—JOHN MAXWELL

CHAPTER SIX

PRINCIPLE 4:
THE PEOPLE PRINCIPLE

The Right People **INFLUENCE** Phenomenal Performance

WHO DO YOU HAVE AROUND YOU?

During the California Gold Rush, a group of eighty-seven people left Missouri to join the wagon train bound for the new opportunities of the West, and in the case of the Donner Party, for a better climate. Along the way, the Donner Party decided to break off from the bigger group and follow a supposedly newly discovered route to significantly shorten the journey. They had purchased a popular map of the new route and followed it specifically. The only problem was the man who created and sold the map had never actually traveled the route!

There were areas where the ground was too soft for the heavy wagons, so they got stuck and had to dig the wagons out of the mush. Axles were broken trying to cross rugged terrain;

instead of saving time, they lost time—a *lot* of time. In fact, Old Man Winter trapped them in the snowcapped mountains that stood between them and their "promised land." They ran out of food and half the party died from starvation. Some of them even resorted to cannibalism to survive.

They took advice from the wrong person! The People Principle is perhaps the most important of all the principles because it influences how you think, what you believe, and ultimately your performance more than anything else. You can have a compelling picture of the future, you can understand your potential, and you can know your purpose—but if you don't have the right people around you, you won't reach your biggest dreams and goals.

In fact, having the right people around you will help you see your potential and the possibilities for your life and business. This has been true for me—the greatest life lesson I have ever learned is to get around people who are already where I want to be. People who have already done what I want to do and have the kind of life I want to have. I want to be around people who are wise, so I can be wise. I want to be around people who have the character I want to have.

If we want to be healthier, we need to be around healthy people. If we want to be smart, we should hang around smart people. If we want to be successful financially, we need to learn from people who are successful financially. If we want to be a better family member, we should spend time with strong families. If we want to be stronger spiritually, we should hang around people who are strong in their faith.

No matter who you hang around, you'll adopt their habits and lifestyle. Research clearly proves this. Authors Darren Hardy, Gary Keller, Jim Rohn, Charlie "Tremendous" Jones, and many others have written about this fact. When Scripture says, "Bad company corrupts good morals," it's not just a religious saying. Hanging around the wrong people will definitely influence you in the wrong way.

This is so true that I was tempted to make this the first principle. The fact is that having the right people around you will help you see a more compelling picture of the future, they will help you understand your potential, and they will help you find your purpose.

My early mentor Bill Beckham was one of the most influential men in my life. He has a way of encouraging people like no one I've ever seen. As a veteran missionary who spent forty years in the mission field, and a pastor since he was eighteen years old, this eighty-year-old man has poured a great deal of wisdom into my life. He helped me see a more positive picture for my life, what my gifts and talents were, and he helped me get the right perspective on life.

I talk a lot about this in my book *The Power of Community.* I share that every human being needs support, encouragement, and accountability to reach their full potential. We need support in every area of our lives to *have* the things we want to have. We need encouragement to *do* the things we may be afraid to do. And we need accountability to *be* the person we want to be. No one is as successful as we could be, without having the right people around us.

Who are the people we need surrounding us?

1. The right faith community
2. The right family members
3. The right consultants, coaches, and mentors
4 The right peers
5. The right team members

I listed faith members first, because our relationship with God will not be as strong as it could be without the support, encouragement, and accountability that come from a strong community of faith. In fact, it was my faith community that helped me become a better family member, leader, and business owner.

Second is a strong foundation at home. I certainly wouldn't be the person I am without my phenomenal wife, Denise. We've been married for thirty-five years, and she has stood by me all these years. Denise is an amazing person. She is loyal, faithful to me and her family. She works extremely hard. She is good with money and makes sure that everyone is taken care of. She shows amazing love to strangers, and she has been my rock throughout the years. Zig said, "When things are good at home, they will be better out in the marketplace." Someone said, "No amount of success can compensate for failure at home."

I don't know about you, but I've lived that one. I spent too much time at the church building, too much time at work, and too much time pursuing my own personal desires to the point that it affected my family life.

Third, we need consultants, coaches, and mentors if we want to perform at the highest level. What professional athlete or entertainer would try to perform without a coach? Neither should we! In our careers and in business, we need the right coaches in our lives.

We not only need people who are where we want to be, we need people who know how to help us get to where we want to go. When my first business wasn't successful, I began learning from others who were successful in business and taught courses on how to be successful. I decided that there would not be one thing in that industry that I did not know. I made the commitment to find the answer to *every* question possible.

As a result, my first company became the top company in that industry in my city and an inspiration to the entire industry worldwide. Many years ago, that business wasn't profitable and I had a ton of debt. I hired financial consultant Ellen Rohr to help me fix it. Then I hired Scott Zack to manage my money for me. As a result, that business is super profitable and I'm debt free.

I became a successful international business coach and mentor by learning from successful mentors and coaches. I hired Rick Jones, who was with Dale Carnegie for thirty-three years and owned the award-winning Houston franchise for more than twenty years. He has not only been where I want to be, and not only have I learned so much about the training business from him, he supports me, encourages me, and helps me stay accountable to my vision. Rick became like a father to me. He is my coach, my mentor.

I began to learn from countless speakers, coaches, and trainers. I began to study the most successful business trainers in America to learn their business model and to see what worked and what didn't work. I hired many of them to speak on my stage and to mentor me. One of those men was Zig Ziglar himself.

Speaking of Zig, his book *Born to Win* has a chapter titled Get the Right Advice, in which he outlines a seven-point criteria for choosing a coach:

1. They have good character.

2. They have a track record of success.

3. They are good listeners.

4. They are good decision makers.

5. They tell the truth, even when it hurts.

6. They have good personal relationships.

7. They celebrate the success of others.

PARTICIPATE

I've observed an interesting phenomenon in our coaching community. When people are struggling, they stop showing up to their coaching sessions. Although they should do just the opposite, it is human nature to try to figure things out ourselves before getting help. In Gary Keller's book *The ONE Thing*, he and coauthor Jay Papasan share research that reveals that "Individuals with written goals and *weekly accountability* are more than 79% more likely to reach those goals."

Your community should be your constant companion. Incidentally, our most successful members are those who simply learn our proven processes and implement them. What makes them implement consistently? They are the ones who attend all of the training sessions and follow through with their coaching calls!

Don't be like the alcoholic who only engages when there is a crisis, *stay* in a constant environment of community so you will remain whole. When you stay plugged into your community, the temptation to drift is minimized. We need to have *built-in* support, encouragement, and accountability on a daily and weekly basis.

Finally, if you are in a leadership role or you own a business, you must have a phenomenal team to have phenomenal performance. If you have a dream (a compelling picture), but you don't have a team (the right people), you have to give up the dream or build up the team.

Early in my career, I was not the best leader of my business. I had passion, phenomenal customer service, and I demanded excellence from my employees, but I went about it in all the wrong ways. I was aggressive, sometimes mean, and plain immature. I got what I wanted at the moment, but not long term.

When I began to learn leadership skills, everything changed. I learned that leadership is effectively communicating your vision. I learned that leadership is a relationship. I learned that by helping my team members get what they wanted out of life, I would get what I wanted. Zig's most famous quote is, "You can have everything in life you want, if you just help enough other people get what they want."

I learned that Personality Profiles are vitally important. The DISC Model of Human Behavior (if you get the assessments from the right source) can make a huge difference. How can you lead if you are speaking a different language? Get a free report on the DISC Model of Human Behavior and purchase a Personality Report at www.HowardPartridge.com/disc.

I learned that meaningful work equals a meaningful life. People spend a lot of time at work, and if they don't have a job they love, they aren't going to be very happy or as productive as they could be. So, it's really important to understand their personality profile and place them in a role in which they can thrive. When people can use their gifts and the environment is supportive and positive, they will produce more, and they will deliver a better product or service.

How well you perform as a leader has a direct impact on the performance of the team, which has a direct impact on the overall performance of the business. You cannot do everything yourself. I get a lot done because I have forty team members who love their work. Do what you do best. Delegate the rest.

To recap, we need a strong personal life. We need people around us who will help us make wise choices. We need mentors and coaches in our personal and professional lives, and if we are going to hit really big goals and live big dreams, we need a phenomenal team. Your team may or may not be employees, but you need a network of people to help you get where you want to go.

Again, having the right people around you will help you get a compelling picture for your life and will help you understand your potential and your purpose. And having the right people around you will help you plan for the future as well, which is the next principle.

ACTION STEPS

1. Review the Goal-Setting Instructions on pages 8 and 9 in your *Ziglar Personal Performance Planner.* Pay special attention to Step 5: Individuals, Groups, Companies and Organizations to Work with to Reach This Goal.

2. Participate in your weekly POD.

Surround yourself with people who are already where you want to be in business and life—and who know how to get you where you want to go.

—HOWARD PARTRIDGE

Do what you do best. Delegate the rest.

—UNKNOWN

You can have everything in life you want, if you will just help enough other people get what they want.

—ZIG ZIGLAR

Where there is no guidance the people fall. But in abundance of counselors there is victory.

—PROVERBS 11:14 NASB

Without consultation, plans are frustrated, but with many counselors they succeed.

—PROVERBS 15:22 NASB

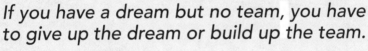

When things are better at home, things will be better in the marketplace. I call that the home court advantage.

—ZIG ZIGLAR

If you have a dream but no team, you have to give up the dream or build up the team.

—DAVE ANDERSON

Individuals with written goals and weekly accountability are 79% more likely to reach those goals.

—GARY KELLER

CHAPTER SEVEN

PRINCIPLE 5: THE PLANNING PRINCIPLE

Proper Planning **INITIATES** Phenomenal Performance

HOW WILL YOU GET THERE?

Have you ever used a Global Positioning System (GPS) to give you directions to a particular destination? It's an amazing tool we have today. There was a time in my life when GPS devices didn't exist for the average civilian. We had to use a paper map! Denise and I have traveled the world since we got married in 1984, so I've used *lots* of maps in my day. But I didn't always follow them accurately.

For example, one summer we drove from Houston to South Padre Island for the first time. As I looked at the map, I *assumed* that we could get to South Padre Island from North Padre Island. And we could drive along the beach at sunset. Makes sense, right? Wrong. We ended up on a dirt road in the middle of the night *on the beach!* As the mice scurried across the sand at the unusual sight of headlights, I finally succumbed to Denise's unhappiness. We turned around. That assumption cost us a *lot* of time.

Paper maps can be deceiving. While in Maui once, I got on the road to Hana by accident. It looked good on the map, but I didn't realize it was a 64-mile-long road that takes *two and a half hours* to drive *one* way! With approximately 620 curves, 59 one-lane bridges and a road so narrow that we couldn't get off it or turn around without endangering our lives, there was no choice but to journey on to Hana. The t-shirts I had seen at the tourist shops featuring an image of a frazzled individual with the caption "I Survived the Road to Hana," now made sense.

Then I made a decision that was *worse* than the accident of getting on that wicked road to start with. Looking at the map, again I *assumed* the only other way out of Hana *had* to be better than the way we came in. This road didn't have curves and fantastic flora and waterfalls, rather it was a never-ending stretch of barren, rocky, dusty, lava-laden road that looked more like Mars than planet Earth! This desolate road, most likely used exclusively by native Hawaiians, went on for miles; dried red clay with a sparse arrangement of large rocks that constantly threatened a flat tire was a poor choice indeed. Thank God we had plenty of gas.

On another occasion, we had a one-day layover in Paris and wanted to see the Eiffel Tower. We were staying at a hotel next to the airport and after sightseeing we took the last train back to the airport. It was after 11 p.m. when everyone got off the train at the stop before the airport. The announcements were in French, so I didn't understand what was being said. Once again, I assumed. I assumed that everyone on the train were locals, and we were the only tourists on that sparsely populated train. However, when the train arrived at the airport, instead of stopping to let passengers off, in this case, just us, it pulled into the dimly lit train yard where all the trains were parked.

To our surprise, the conductor, got off the train without letting us off. Our surprise turned to horror when all the lights went off and the doors automatically locked us in like a prison cell! Yelling and screaming, banging on the windows, we tried to get the conductor's attention, but he obviously couldn't see us or hear us. Finished with his work day, he walked toward the airport building. We were immediately faced with the dreaded prospect of sleeping on the hard, cold, metal floor of that train all night.

As we continued to plead, pray, and pound on the windows, desperately hoping the conductor would hear us before he slipped into the shadows for good, he finally turned to take one last look at his train. Perhaps to double-check that he had completely powered down. Or perhaps prompted by human nature, or our desperate prayer had fell on God's ears, he saw us. Looking a little surprised and confused, he hurried over and unlocked the train.

Although I still get grief from Denise about these few instances, she would be the first to confess that my overall record over the years has had *many* more wins than losses. From navigating the roundabouts in Amsterdam full of people on bicycles, street cars, buses, and taxis driving on the street car rails, not to mention hordes of pedestrians, to driving on the left-hand side of the road, whether in England or Australia, to the cliff-side roads of Greece in a stick-shift rental car, I've driven us many, many places successfully.

Today, it's much easier with this amazing technology called GPS. Reaching your biggest dreams and goals is like traveling to a destination you've never been. The analogy of a trip to an amazing destination is a good one for the principle of planning.

As I write this piece, we are on our fourth trip to Italy. The first trip was for our twentieth wedding anniversary fifteen years ago, so we had a big reason to go. It was a really big deal for Denise, and we still talk about the trip to this day. Of course, we had to decide exactly where we wanted to go in the country. I had to research where to stay. I had to plan flights, trains, and arrange other transportation. There were tickets to buy for certain attractions, and of course we had to pay for the trip.

As we review the principles of phenomenal performance, did we have the potential to go? Of course! But would you be surprised to learn that people who really want to go to Hawaii or Italy don't go, even though they have the desire and they have the means? Maybe they're afraid to fly. Maybe, they're worried about being away. Maybe they fear what their average thinking family, coworkers, or neighbors might think of them for doing something so crazy.

Is the *picture* principle in play here? Of course! We imagine all the wonderful things we will experience, and this is the most exciting part! Why don't we apply that principle to our *greatest* journey? Our *life* journey!

Did we have a *purpose* to go? Yes. It was our twentieth wedding anniversary. Why are we on this trip to Italy now? Our son and daughter-in-love are celebrating their first wedding anniversary, and we are celebrating our thirty-fifth. Obviously, the only reason you need to go somewhere is a desire to go, but that in itself is a purpose.

Do you need the assistance of other *people* to go someplace exciting you've never been before? Absolutely! Whether you get advice from friends who have been there, or you get advice from an expert. You might even have an official tour guide on your trip. What you *don't* want to do is get advice from someone who has never been or someone who doesn't have the same interests as you.

The Planning Principle is key not only for travel, but for life and business. We need a roadmap. We need a GPS. In my book *The 5 Secrets of a Phenomenal Business*, GPS is identified as:

Goals

Plans

Systems

First, we have to have *goal*. That's the picture. Then we have to have a *plan*. That is your route. S is for *systems*. A system is a group of working parts that when operating together, duplicate results consistently.

A vehicle is a system made up of several systems. So far, as we've traveled to Italy, we took a car to the airport, a shuttle bus from parking to the airport, a big plane to Frankfurt, a shuttle bus from the terminal to a smaller plane, a taxi from the Florence airport to the hotel. We walked everywhere in

Florence, except one evening when we took a rickshaw from the piazza to our hotel. Taxi to the airport to meet our Tuscany group, loaded into a van and off to the Tuscan castle. Then a rental car was used to tour the countryside.

How well your trip goes is a direct result of how well you plan. Success doesn't happen by accident. It's by *design*. You need a *map*. It has been said that "Planning a journey without a map is like building a house without a blueprint." Jesus Himself said that only a fool would build a tower without a plan.

Whether you reach your goals or not, depends on proper planning. I heard it said that "A goal without a plan is just a wish." You've probably also heard "Failing to plan is planning to fail." I agree with that. Many people cringe at the idea of planning. For me, I've come to love it. I love ideas, and I've learned that if those ideas are going to become a reality, I have to plan.

One more great quote about planning: "Proper planning and preparation prevents poor performance." And that is what this book is all about. We can turn that statement into the positive as well. "Proper planning and preparation promotes phenomenal performance." Zig said you were born to win, but in order to be the winner you were born to be, you must *plan* to win and *prepare* to win.

Planning means laying out the steps to reach the goal. *Preparing* means making sure you have the resources, the knowledge, the contacts, and the provisions to make the trip. It also means fleshing it out. It means testing, tweaking, and training to win. Preparing is practicing. Train as hard as you fight. Training breeds confidence. Learning, practicing, and testing is key to phenomenal performance.

Planning helps you focus. Planning *initiates* phenomenal performance because it forces you to think through the steps. What are the steps that need to be taken to accomplish the goal? When planning my trip to Italy, we first needed an *itinerary* before I could even order tickets.

Your plan is your itinerary. Your itinerary outlines each step along the way. One of the best ways to do this is to clearly define your end goal or your vision. The better defined it is, the more likely you can create an itinerary. If you don't really know where you are going, you can't really create an itinerary!

In order for your GPS to work, it must also know *where* you are starting from. If you have a sales goal, where are you starting from? If you have a growth goal, what are your current statistics? The *Wheel of Life Assessment* helps you identify where you are compared to where you want to be in life. Our *Wheel of Business Assessment* helps you identify where your business is currently, compared to where you want it to be. If you want to improve your health, you need to know what healthy stats look like and where you are currently. Identifying your current condition is the starting point.

From your assessments, you can then set appropriate goals. Once you've identified your goals, you can properly plan. Your plan starts with your dream. You might call this your "Someday Goal" as Gary Keller, cofounder of Keller-Williams, the largest residential real estate company in the United States, says in his blockbuster book *The ONE Thing—The Surprisingly Simple Truth Behind Extraordinary Results.*

You then turn your Someday Goal into a five-year goal. In light of your someday goal, where do you need to be in five years? Then you chunk that goal down to a one-year goal. Where do you need to be in a year? Then you chunk that down to a monthly goal, then a weekly goal, a daily goal, and finally a *right now* goal, which leads to our next principle: The Priority Principle.

The story from the Gold Rush era about the Donner party that I shared earlier shows how not having the right plan can wipe out an entire family group. Would planning your life better and more intentionally create a more lasting and meaningful legacy for your family? Absolutely. Would better planning help you build the career or business you really want? Absolutely! And the lack thereof can be disastrous.

Proper planning is wise. Being humble enough to admit you don't have all the answers, and just winging it won't get you where you want to go. In his book *Leading with Questions: How Leaders Find the Right Solutions by Knowing What to Ask,* author Michael J. Marquardt shares how pride, denial, and ego led to the sinking of The Titanic, the explosion of the space shuttle Challenger, and the fall of Enron. In each of these cases, the arrogance, pride, and ego of the individuals involved led to disasters that had worldwide impact. Not to mention the obstinate denial of the facts.

You may not feel that your life, your career, or your business is as important as these incidents, but you would be wrong. If you feel that way, you might want to go back to the first principle, The Potential Principle, to understand how important your life is. How do you know whether or not your son, daughter, or grandchild will be the next president of the United States? How do you know whether or not your child, relative, or employee will become the next Billy Graham or Nelson Mandela?

You don't. But what I hope you *do* know is that you are valuable to God, and your purpose is as important as anyone else's. Your life is precious. Your life is worth planning! The level of your performance depends on your level of planning! And your business and career are no different. Your business or career is important enough to plan for because it impacts many other people.

ACTION STEPS

1. Set four goals on pages 10–12 in your *Ziglar Personal Performance Planner.* You have to have a destination to get started! Set four goals or projects and work through the seven steps.

2. Participate in your weekly POD.

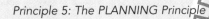

You were born to win, but in order to be the winner you were born to be, you must plan to win and prepare to win before you can expect to win.

—ZIG ZIGLAR

Failing to plan is planning to fail.

—ALAN LAKEIN

Proper planning and preparation prevents poor performance.

—STEPHEN KEAGUE

A goal without a plan is just a wish.

—ANTOINE DE SAINT-EXUPERY

The plans of the diligent lead surely to abundance, but everyone who is hasty comes only to poverty.

—PROVERBS 21:5 ESV

CHAPTER EIGHT

PRINCIPLE 6: THE PRIORITY PRINCIPLE

Living by Priority **IGNITES** Phenomenal Performance

WHAT'S IMPORTANT NOW?

There's a little seafood market in Destin named Goatfeathers. What a strange name. What is a *goat* feather? Goats don't have feathers! It turns out that *Goatfeathers* is the name of a personal development book from all the way back to 1812, written by Ellis Parker Butler. "Goatfeathers you understand, are the feathers a man picks and sticks all over his hide to make himself look like the village goat," the author pens.

Butler continues, "Goatfeathers are the distractions, sidelines and deflections that take a man's attention from his own business and keep him from getting ahead. They are the greatest thing in the world to make a man look like a goat. The time we waste in excursions off the main line of our road to our goal is the difference between success and have success. Often, it is the difference between success and failure."

PERSPICACIOUS

Many years ago, the guest speaker at one of my conferences was NASA astronaut and head of the spacewalk program, Dr. David Wolf. Dr. Wolf has been on four shuttle missions and has had a remarkable career. One of my colleagues who introduced him to me was writing a book on words of success. He asked each successful person he knew to describe the most important power word for success.

Dr. Wolf's answer was "perspicacious." Admittedly, I didn't know what the word meant, and I hoped my friend would keep him occupied long enough for me to look up the definition. In essence, it means to stay focused in the midst of all the potential distractions around you. Think of the movie *Gravity* starring Sandra Bullock and George Clooney. An explosion of space junk was coming at them at a fast rate of speed. They had to stay focused to survive.

Today's culture offers so many distractions with social media and entertainment. Also, there are so many things to do, life itself can be overwhelming. The key is to prioritize your tasks. We must constantly ask ourselves the question, *What's important now?*

You may have seen the "Big Rock, Little Rock" demonstration. There are a few big rocks that represent your biggest priorities for the day. Little rocks represent the things you have to do, but aren't as important as the big rocks. Pebbles represent another set of things you have to do, but are even less important than the little rocks. Then comes the sand. Sand represents an even lesser important group of activities. Let's call that social media. And water represents things that are a complete waste of time, like getting sucked into an endless loop of Facebook videos, or getting hooked on a Netflix series that you can't stop watching, which really doesn't add any value to you.

Now, let's imagine you have a jar. Let's pour the water in first. Then the sand, then the pebbles, then the little rocks. There is no room for the big rocks! And this actually happens to many people!

But when you put the big rocks, the most important priority projects, in first, instead of the most urgent, you can get the most important things done. Just because someone needs you doesn't mean you have to react right away. I love the little meme that states, "Your lack of planning doesn't constitute an emergency on my part!"

When you get the big rocks out of the way first, you'll accomplish your biggest goals. As the old Southern saying goes, "If the hardest thing you have to do today is eat a frog, then by all means do it first and get it out of the way!" Brian Tracy wrote an entire book titled *Eat That Frog*. It's an international best seller. Why? Because *everyone* suffers from FTI from one degree to another. We can *all* be tempted to get distracted by less important things.

Next, you put in the little rocks. They will work their way into the spaces between the big rocks. Maybe these are important phone calls or emails that need to be made today. The pebbles come next. They will work themselves into the spaces around the little rocks. Then comes the sand. It's so fine that it will find its way into the tiny spaces around the pebbles. Finally, you pour the water in the jar and it soaks into the sand.

One time I was coaching a guy who was not as successful as he could have been in his business. He had way more potential than he was tapping into, and he felt stuck. I began to ask him about his daily routine. "How do you use your mornings?" I asked.

"I do crossword puzzles," he sheepishly confessed.

CROSSWORD PUZZLES?! I thought to myself. I couldn't get over it. I was absolutely flabbergasted that a *businessman* would spend his precious, miracle morning time with such an activity! No *wonder* he was stuck! The truth is that he was not a businessman, he was a technician who owned a business, who was just getting through the day.

PROJECTS

The key to The Priority Principle is to identify specific projects that will help you reach your goal. I suggest you have four priority projects. I call them the Phenomenal Four. These are the big rocks. These are the four things that will have the biggest impact on your life, your career, or your business. One of those projects will be your top priority that trumps all others.

For example, let's say that you're a business owner and you're not profitable, or you're not sure if you are or not. That becomes your number one priority project. If a business isn't profitable, it won't be a business for very long. You would identify this as a project and act on it every day.

One of my clients, Mike Killen, who is in our Inner Circle Coaching Program, had this problem. When he first came to me two years ago, his business was sucking money out of his savings account at a very rapid pace. He was scared to death. On top of that, he had a number of personnel issues.

Mike's top priority project was to know his company's financial position ("known financial position" or KFP as my friend and consultant Ellen Rohr calls it). Even though it took him over a year to complete this project, it transformed his business. Today, his sales are at a record high and his profits are at an all-time high.

Mike told me that he has more money in his bank accounts than ever in his life. Meanwhile, his leadership has improved and therefore his team has improved and he took his family on the vacation of a lifetime. Not only did he implement, he prioritized his activities.

It's all about focus. Gary Keller's book *The ONE Thing* revolves around a phenomenal question—the focusing question. This question helps you identify the one, most important thing that will give you extraordinary results in each area of your life and business. Here's the question: "What's the one thing I can do such that by doing it everything else will be easier or unnecessary?"

What was the *one* thing Mike Killen had to do to fix his financial situation? Know the company's financial position. What was the *one* thing Mike had to do to get to KFP? Set up his accounting systems. What was the *one* thing Mike had to do to set up the accounting systems? Hire someone. What was the *one* thing Mike had to do to hire someone?

Can you see how taking your biggest priority and drilling down to the *one*, most important task can have a *huge* impact? Are things easier for Mike today? You bet! Are some things unnecessary? YES! He doesn't have to worry about money for one thing. Unnecessary. Does he have to transfer money from his savings to make payroll? Unnecessary!

Notice that the question contains this phrase "such that by *doing* it." That's called *implementation!*

You can apply the One Thing philosophy to every area of life or business:

- "What's the ONE thing I can do for my family life..."
- "What's the ONE thing I can do for my key relationships..."
- "What's the ONE thing I can do for my finances..."
- "What's the ONE thing I can do for my health..."
- "What's the ONE thing I can do for my spiritual life..."

In his hugely popular book *The 7 Habits of Highly Successful People,* the late Steven Covey taught us the difference between the urgent and the important. He actually created a table that had these quadrants:

- Important and Urgent
- Important and Not Urgent
- Not Important But Urgent
- Not Important and Not Urgent

Examples:

- Important and Urgent: Your most important client is waiting on the phone with a problem on an important project

- Important and Not Urgent: Your tax return needs to be filed, but it's not due for a while

- Not Important But Urgent: Someone is demanding your attention to tell you a funny joke

- Not Important and Not Urgent: Watching Facebook videos

PRUNING

As you track your time, and you become more aware of how you are using your time, you'll want to ask yourself whether you're doing too much yourself. Is it time to delegate some things? Is it time to eliminate some things? You can't do everything yourself and continue to grow. *Pruning* is an essential gardening skill. When you prune correctly, you encourage healthy growth.

Use a Time Log for two weeks to track what you are working on and when. Simply pause for a minute or two every hour and jot down what you worked on that hour in your *Ziglar Personal Performance Planner*. There is a section called the *Personal Performance Record* where you record your activity.

Start from the time you get up and continue until you go to bed. Do it for two weeks, and you'll begin to see what your priorities are. You'll also see your pattern of activity, which will come into play in The Productivity Principle. And, you'll see whether you just have too much on your plate or not. It may be time to delegate some of your tasks as we talked about in The People Principle.

Remember these words from Gary Keller, "Achievers always work from a sense of priority." In order to stay focused, we need to prioritize. In order to stay focused on our priorities and to act on them, we need accountability. Make sure you have the right people around you to help you stay accountable to what's important right now.

It's so easy to get distracted. It's so easy to eat the wrong thing when trying to get healthy. It's so easy to do what you want to do, rather than what you should do. What is your *one* thing? What is your *one thing* in your life? What is your *one thing* in your career? What is your *one thing* in your business?

So many people get distracted by bright shiny objects. I expect my ten-month-old granddaughter to get distracted easily. In fact, I intentionally distract her with a brightly colored toy when I need to. But as adults who have the capacity to critically think in order to perform in the areas of life and business that are important to us, we should be able to look past distractions and keep on task.

PLEASURE

Many years ago, I did some amateur photography and got pretty good at it. This was during the days of film, before cameras went digital. I had begun to lose interest and let that hobby go by the wayside. I love to take pictures, and it's incredible what you can do with just an iPhone, but recently my son encouraged me to get a new camera, mainly because the camera has 4K video to shoot content videos.

I brought the camera along on the Italy trip and had a blast shooting the amazing architecture, vineyards, sunflower fields, and the sheer beauty of Tuscany. My son noticed how happy I was when photographing and encouraged me to take up the hobby again.

It's important to have fun, but I'm not interested in investing a lot of time in that hobby because of the time it would take away from more important things. Will I take pictures on vacation? Yes. Will I play around with some photography after I'm finished with my most important work? Yes. Will I invest some of my rest day taking some photos when I'm in a beautiful or interesting place? Yes! In fact, recently I drove from Destin to Mississippi to visit some family members. The back roads of Alabama and Mississippi were dotted with old tractors and trucks that would have made phenomenal photos. I could easily have spent a few entire days photographing along those roads.

But as Zig warned: "The chief cause of failure and unhappiness is trading what you want most for what you want now." What's important now? What should you really be focused on right now to take you where you want to go in your life? In your career? In your business?

We have so many choices, and in our pleasure-seeking culture, we can perhaps put too much emphasis on having fun and neglect the things that will make a difference in the world. Zig laughed heartily at the question, "How many of you have noticed that people who have nothing to do, want to do it with you?"

In fact, the first time I interviewed Zig Ziglar, I was curious why he would take the time to do a video interview in the studio with me at that point in his career. He received $100,000 per speech, usually traveled on a private jet, and didn't need the money. He was in his early eighties at the time. He had given plenty.

I knew he had a lake house close by that he loved to spend time with the Redhead (the nickname he gave his wife, Jean). "Mr. Ziglar, I know you have a lake house nearby that you and your wife love spending time. Why are you doing this interview with me? Aren't there more pleasurable things you could be doing right now?" I asked. I'll never forget his response.

"There may be more pleasurable things I could be doing right now, but there are few things that are more important," Zig said.

Here's a warning: When you live on purpose for a long time, eventually the purpose has *you* rather than *you* having a purpose. In other words, it takes over. Does that mean you don't have any fun? Does it mean that you can't take time off? Not at all! In fact, taking time to have fun is required to recharge. In order to achieve phenomenal performance to reach your phenomenal picture, you have to stay proactive and focused. Folly is not the goal. If you want to be fulfilled and have deep joy in your life, live on purpose and live by priority.

ACTION STEPS

1. Read pages 13-17 in your *Ziglar Personal Performance Planner.* In this section, you learn how to fill out the Weekly Activity Record and *Personal Performance Record.*

2. Fill out your first week of the *Personal Performance Record* on pages 18 and 19 of your planner.

3. Participate in your weekly POD.

Achievers always work from a sense of priority.
—GARY KELLER

The chief cause of failure and unhappiness is trading what you want most for what you want now.
—ZIG ZIGLAR

If you aim at nothing, you will hit it every time.
—ZIG ZIGLAR

Goatfeathers are the distractions, sidelines and deflections that take a man's attention from his own business and keep him from getting ahead.
—ELLIS PARKER BUTLER

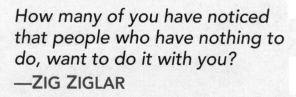

How many of you have noticed that people who have nothing to do, want to do it with you?
—ZIG ZIGLAR

What's the one thing I can do, such that by doing it, everything else becomes easier or unnecessary?
—GARY KELLER

Most people are a wandering generality rather than a meaningful specific.
—ZIG ZIGLAR

People often complain about lack of time when the lack of direction is the real problem.
—ZIG ZIGLAR

CHAPTER NINE

PRINCIPLE 7:
THE PROCESS PRINCIPLE

A Simple Process **IMPROVES**
Phenomenal Performance

WHAT SYSTEMS WILL YOU USE?

Several years ago, I had the opportunity to visit the Boeing aircraft plant in Seattle. They even allowed our group to tour the assembly floor. At the time, Boeing was building the very first *787 Dreamliner.* The assembly of this vehicle was different from previous aircraft. Instead of building it part by part at the Boeing plant, several nations each built a complete component of the aircraft, and then shipped it to Boeing. The Rolls Royce engines were built in England, of course; the wings were built in Japan. Italy created one of the fuselages; France did the passenger doors; cargo doors were Swedish; Korea made the wingtips; and everything else was manufactured somewhere in the United States. The huge components sat separately on the assembly floor. Then each was connected.

As mentioned earlier, a system is a group of working parts that duplicate results consistently. I often tell business owners that their business is a vehicle to help them reach their life goals. If you are an employee, your job is the vehicle you have chosen to reach *your* life goals.

The purpose of a vehicle is to take you somewhere! Where do you want to go? Some people have a lot of dreams and need lots of vehicles—businesses or income streams. I'm one of those people. I wanted to go somewhere new so I started Phenomenal Products even though I already had a successful business. I invest in real estate and have various partnerships to add money, resources, and tools to my portfolio. The kind of vehicle(s) you use make it possible to go further. The 787 Dreamliner will take a lot of people a long way!

My friend David Frey taught me this acronym for SYSTEM:

Save

Your

Self

Time

Energy

Money

A simple system saves you time, therefore you can get more done in less time. A simple system saves you energy, therefore you can get more done before your willpower meter runs low.

Simple systems save you money because you avoid wasting materials doing something over and over.

In my companies, we have certain ways that we do things that have been proven the most effective, therefore saving us labor cost of a task taking too long or having to redo it. My service company in Houston is completely turnkey. It generates several million dollars per year, and I have a team in place that simply runs the simple processes that we created many years ago. They still work wonderfully well today! That company is *very* predictable, another benefit of systems, and very profitable. I created a leadership system that keeps team members long term, which creates predictability on the employee side. There are thirty-three team members at that company.

We've created marketing and sales systems that create predictable income. We've created operations systems to keep everything running smoothly and administration systems to keep the profits predictable. Our leadership systems keep the culture in check.

My friend and fellow consultant Ellen Rohr says, "The simpler you make it the farther you can take it." Most of my work is helping small business owners build systems in their businesses. If you are a business owner and you have not yet connected with us about your business, go to www.HowardPartridge.com and opt in to get free business growth strategies.

At my coaching and training company, Phenomenal Products, I write books, speak at conferences, conduct at least twenty workshops per year, and host four major conferences of my own. I travel the world, lead a number of weekly webinars myself, and deliver a number of one-on-one coaching sessions.

Plus, I participate in a number conference calls with partners and potential partners.

We coach in 109 different industries in twenty countries, and I help Tom Ziglar run the Zig Ziglar Corporation and Ziglar, Inc. I oversee all aspects of that business, and I also have a few LLC structured companies, including investment real estate, a little software company I recently purchased, a franchise agreement, and things like that. Does all of this keep me super busy six days a week? Yes!

I couldn't do all of it without my team—The People Principle. My team runs the systems. They handle all the day-to-day functions of my business affairs, but I also have my own Performance Results Description (PRD). My role is to create content, teach, create the vision, direct the team, and build strategic relationships.

Even though I have many responsibilities, I still get seven or eight hours of sleep every night and there is time for exercise, family time, and faith time. As you'll learn later in this book, it's really all about scheduling. I don't work past 4 p.m. except to interact by email or social media—if I want to. I make time to go to the beach and take long walks or a swim. I can take two weeks off to go to Italy without having to be concerned about business affairs. I can choose what I want to do. During my time in Italy, I wasn't contacted by my team. They didn't need me.

We have a scheduling process to keep everything flowing. If I want to be "off," then I simply block my schedule. My assistant even takes care of our home and our animals while we are away. We have specific instructions for her even for that.

We don't just say, "Take care of the house" and get upset if she doesn't do it the way we want it done. There's a *process.*

Even if you don't have a company, you need people and systems in your life too. Every phenomenally successful person needs a phenomenal dream team. That might be a rock-star babysitter, CPA, doctor, or drycleaner. The more you can delegate, the more capacity you can create.

If we want to get *more* done in the *right* way, we need to maximize our time, and we can do that with simple systems. Systems save you time, money, and energy. For example, I have my dry cleaning picked up and delivered. It's easier, takes less time, and the money is probably about the same. I'm saving money since I'm saving time. The cleaners come twice a week and the only thing we need to remember is to put the clothes out for pickup.

I have a process to organize my time, which I will share in a bit. I have a simple process for how I dress. I bought about forty of the same shorts and the same shirts (I work from home), so I don't have to worry about what to wear, or if I have clean clothes or not. I always have more than I need. I can simply go to my closet and grab the same thing every day. I *do* have different colors to choose from, so at least there is *some* variety! If it was up to me, I would wear all white every day. Yes, just call me *Howeird.*

I have an eating system. I have everything I need to make my meals every day. I don't have to decide where I'm going to lunch, or what I want to eat. It's already there. Eating the same exact thing every single day drives my wife crazy! But it saves me time, money, and energy!

I have the same routine six days a week. I get up at the same time and go to bed at the same time, if possible. I do certain things on certain days. For example, on Saturday I run my business numbers. I review my income statements and marketing reports from my companies and tweak the marketing messages for the following week, if needed.

I have specific meetings on specific days. For example, every Monday we have a team meeting, a phenomenal products via video. On Tuesdays I deliver my weekly Inner Circle webcast. I have a couple of leadership groups I lead, and a book-writing group I colead. They are simply blocked on a recurring calendar.

My assistant, Michelle, is responsible for scheduling a substitute in advance if I cannot be present due to my travel schedule.

I don't work on Sundays. I go to church, spend time with my family, sometimes play basketball, and do things around the house. I don't want to sacrifice worship for my job, and I don't want to waste precious time during the week doing chores that don't contribute to my overall goals.

I do certain things at certain times. After coffee in the morning, the first thing I do is read. I read a few pages from whatever book I'm reading, and then I read a chapter from the Scriptures every day. Then I pray. I have a specific process of prayer that includes certain things.

Then I work on my priority projects, which may include planning an event, writing a book, or updating my marketing systems. I may write for several hours, build a presentation deck, or I may sit in the sun with a spiral notebook and work things out on paper first.

I have specific blocks on my calendar for my webcasts, writing, interviews, and things like that. I don't take phone calls until the afternoon, because my creative energy is strongest in the morning. I make my appointments forty-five minutes long so I have time to check email in between calls. I like to keep up on my email throughout the day, unlike twice per day, like some productivity gurus espouse. I feel that if I respond to emails right away, whoever it is I am responding to can get more done themselves.

I do all my personal banking online and I only pay my bills once a month. I have a little stack of my regular bills and I process them once a month. It takes only a few minutes each month. Why would I take the time write checks and put them in an envelope? I'm debt free, but I still have utility bills, and things of that nature.

I have another little stack for my investment statements. Once a month, I simply update the balances so I always have a current personal financial statement ready if my bank needs it for their files, or I decide to make a real estate investment.

When I'm in the car, I use that time to make phone calls. I drive the Houston-Destin track often, and if it's on a weekday, I may be on the phone most of the day. If not, I use that time for thinking.

There are only certain things that I personally do. I have a team that does everything else. We use a tool called a PRD (Performance Results Description). Instead of a job description, it outlines the results required for the position and the performance required to reach those results.

Most people are overwhelmed because they don't have processes. A process takes the pressure off the person. You can try to be Superman or Wonder Woman if you want, but you'll get more done and you'll take it farther faster with simple systems. The simpler you make it, the farther you can take it.

When I use online banking and do it all it once, it saves me an incredible amount of time. In his book *The ONE Thing*, Gary Keller warns us about multitasking. Research has clearly shown true multitasking is ineffective and can actually cost you time. There is also a "switch cost" when you move your attention from one task to another.

Having my dry cleaning picked up and delivered saves me tons of time and energy.

PRESSURE

A process takes the pressure off people. Simple systems not only reduce the amount of time, money, and energy expended, but can also reduce stress. People often wonder how I get so much done. And they're really surprised when they learn that I don't seem stressed or in a hurry. I don't feel a lot of pressure, and that's because I have a process.

A process helps you delegate too. One of the biggest reasons I can get so much done is because I have a team to whom I delegate tasks. You can't delegate very well if there's no process.

PREDICTABILITY

A system creates predictability. As I mentioned, I grew up on welfare in LA (Lower Alabama!). Mobile, to be exact. There were seven kids crammed into a little 600 square foot shack. The roof on that house was so bad that every time it rained, we had to get the pots and pans out to catch the leaks. My mother fed us on $100 a month from the welfare department.

When you grow up in an environment like that, what are you likely to turn out like? For me, picture a rebellious eighteen-year-old who got kicked out of the house. I deserved it. A series of unfortunate events led to that eventuality. A couple of car wrecks convinced my mama and my step-dad that I wasn't ready to own a car. They were right, but as a teenager, you gotta have wheels, so I went down to the used car lot and bought a 1964 Dodge Coronet for $250.

Even in 1978, you don't get much for that amount of money. The muffler was missing, so it was annoyingly loud. I worked the graveyard shift, and I'm sure my family and the neighbors appreciated when I cranked it up at midnight and roared down the little road we lived on. There were holes in the floorboard, where an awful white smoke from the exhaust flowed into the car. The smoke was so nasty it could choke out the strongest of passengers. Rain or shine, the windows had to be down. Otherwise, I'd die!

The gas gauge didn't work, so my friends and I would rock the car back and forth and listen for any gas sloshing around inside. On graduation night, we lost the guessing game. We ran out of gas on a pitch-black lonely road in the countryside of lower Alabama.

Shortly after that fiasco, the brakes went out and I pulled one of the wheels off to check it out. A dozen parts fell onto the ground. Obviously, the only thing predictable about that vehicle was its unpredictability. It didn't serve me very well; based on its condition, I should not have expected it to!

Let's be clear—the owner of that car needed a lot of work too! I often wonder how it was possible for me to rely on a car like that. Even more baffling is why any sane human being would climb in that rust rocket of a death trap with me!

In your business, in your career, and even in your personal life, you need systems to *improve* your performance. That maroon, Bondo/putty-covered Dodge Coronet did not have good working systems and ended up falling apart before it was all over. I sold it to a junkyard for twenty-five bucks.

A new car, or a well-maintained car, will consistently get you where you need to go. I often rent cars when I travel, and normally they have very low mileage. The last thing the rental car company wants to do is rescue someone because a vehicle broke down.

Think about any kind of vehicle. Whether it's a unicycle or a double-decker passenger jet, it's a system. It's simply a group of working parts that create a process to make that vehicle go. If your vehicle is in good operating order, and someone knows how to operate it, then you can get where you want to go predictably.

Speaking of aviation, in that world, every aircraft is operated according to a simple checklist. There's a checklist before the pilot starts the aircraft, after the engine starts, before takeoff, after takeoff, approach, landing, parking the aircraft, and securing the aircraft. Nothing is left to chance.

PRECISION

A system creates precision. When you duplicate an action precisely, you are sure to get the same result every time. McDonald's fast-food restaurant was the "poster child" for systems. A scene in the movie *The Founder* demonstrated this perfectly. The movie told the story of Ray Kroc, the man who acquired exclusive rights to franchise McDonald's around the world.

The scene showed the employees practicing every movement in the tiny space they had to work in. There was a precise number of pickles on the burger, a precise amount of ketchup, and so on. The precision of the ingredients, the supply chain, and the exact methods created the possibility of getting the same hamburger in Alaska as you do in Alabama as their website states.

It may not be the best hamburger, but it's the same hamburger, because they have simple systems to produce a predictable result. This is the value in having simple systems to operate by in your life, in your job, and in your business.

Systems aren't reserved for low-priced businesses either. The Ritz-Carlton Hotel Company has systems. Tesla has systems. Anything you want to scale has a set of process they use to get more consistent results. You get the same experience at every location.

And that's what implementation is all about—improving your performance to the point you are getting the results you want.

I must mention that automation is an important component in systematizing your life and business. For example, at my companies, we have software that automates scheduling, billing, marketing, and sales and reduces paperwork and time involved.

ACTION STEPS

1. Read pages 128 and 129, the *Important Meetings and Projects Journal* section of your *Ziglar Personal Performance Planner.* Use this section to begin outlining the simple processes you'll need to build. You can use as designed or anyway you like. It's *your* planner. I use this section to outline my business plan and to outline events.

2. If you are a business owner, get *The Howard Partridge Simple Dimple Business Plan* at www .HowardPartridgeInnerCircle.com.

3. Participate in your weekly POD.

A process takes the pressure off the person.
—UNKNOWN

A system is a group of working parts that duplicate results consistently.
—HOWARD PARTRIDGE

The simpler you make it the farther you can take it.
—ELLEN ROHR

CHAPTER TEN

PRINCIPLE 8: THE PRODUCTIVITY PRINCIPLE

Persistent, Consistent Productivity **INSURES** Phenomenal Performance

WHAT ACTION ARE YOU TAKING?

In 2014, I had leadership expert John Maxwell deliver the keynote address at my conference. He opened his talk to the two hundred plus business owners, "If I could have dinner with you, I could predict your future success." I saw more than a few people cross their arms and lean back, suggesting that his statement was arrogant.

He continued, "If we were able to have dinner together tonight, I would ask you about your daily agenda. Your future success is determined by your daily agenda." Arms came uncrossed and pens began to hit the paper. He shared that if you had a tree you wanted to chop down, that you could take down any tree of any size just by giving it five chops a day.

It's true. Taking consistent action every day will insure phenomenal performance. When you understand your potential, have a compelling picture, know your purpose, have the right people around you, plan properly, prioritize your activity, use simple processes, and simply take *persistent, consistent action* every day, you'll end up with phenomenal performance that will help you reach your biggest dreams and goals.

The Productivity Principle is where the "rubber meets the road" so to speak. *This* is implementation. *This* is where it all happens. *This* is what separates the players from the real producers. Allow me take you back to the beginning of this book. The number one reason people don't reach their goals is FTI— Failure To Implement.

If you don't have consistent productivity, you won't have phenomenal performance. It's as simple as that. A Japanese proverb states: "Vision without action is just a daydream. Action without vision is a nightmare." You can have the most spectacular vision ever, but if you don't act, it does you no good. And if you are driven by circumstances every day, there is no telling where you will end up.

Everybody is busy today, but as my good friend Michelle Prince likes to say, "Many people are just busy being *busy*." You might be surprised to find that most people who are highly productive don't describe themselves as "busy." Why? Because they plan. They prepare. They have purpose. They know their potential. They have a compelling picture. They have the right people around them to support them, to encourage them, and to help them be accountable to be the best version of themselves. And they take massive action without feeling stressed about it.

Let's talk about your daily activity. I shared in the last chapter about having simple processes for your life and business. In my book *Think and Be Phenomenal,* I outlined my Personal Organizational System that helps me stay focused and highly productive.

The cornerstone of the system is what I call my *daily time capsule.* This is time you set aside, preferably in the morning before you do anything else. Use this time to focus. Use this time to work on your priority projects. Gary Keller calls this time *strategic thought time.* Others call it their *quiet time.* Whatever you call it, how you start your day usually determines how the rest of your day is going to go. Remember, you must *plan* to win. Living your life by circumstance won't get you where you want to go. Instead, live your life according to a *vision.*

In my daily time capsule, I review my top four priority projects every day and simply determine what the next action step is for that project. The idea is to simply move the ball down the field just a little more each and *every* day, six days a week. That action may be delegating something, doing research, or learning how to do something. Whatever the action step is, the faster you take it, the faster you complete that project.

For example, maybe you're having a new website built, creating a slide deck for a presentation, or you are creating a new procedure for your company or your job. Maybe you're writing a book like I am now.

You need a day of rest too, so decided what day that will be. You may feel that you can't take a day off every week, but you would be wrong. About thirteen years ago, I began to take Sundays off, and I found that I got more done than ever before. Remember the pruning principle.

At the time, I had a personal fitness trainer. I was a few years into this process of taking a full day of rest every week and I shared the concept with her. Like most people, she did not believe she could take a day off. "I have two clients who can *only* train on Sunday," she explained.

"If you tell them you aren't working on Sunday, I *guarantee* they will figure out how to do it during the week. Even if you lose two clients, you can pick up two additional during the week," I rebutted.

She was skeptical, but she had a talk with her two clients and sure enough her clients not only moved to another day, they heartily agreed that she shouldn't have to work seven days a week. For the past decade, Leslie has taken off every Sunday to walk her dog in the park and to rest her body and soul.

You see, the spiritual principle of the Sabbath rest, like *all* spiritual principles, was created for our benefit. God "worked" six days a week as an example for us. Your body, your mind, and your emotions need rest on a weekly basis to keep you fresh, creative, and focused. You were designed that way. If you have family, you may want to set Saturday aside for family.

PLACE

The reason I like to get started early is so that my daily time capsule is not interrupted. No one else is awake. In *The ONE Thing*, Gary Keller encourages us to build a bunker. He suggests stocking your workspace with water, snacks, and all of your supplies so you won't encounter any distractions during the day. In other words, you need to be someplace where no one can interrupt you, and you are not likely to come across "landmines" that will undermine your focus. If you need to go to a coffee shop, park, or the beach—do it!

Avoiding interruptions also includes silencing the notifications on your digital devices and being clear with your staff not to bother you during that time. I've met Gary Keller a couple of times and spent time learning his business model from him. His office is strategically positioned near the front of the building for easy entry and exit. He has a private bathroom, not because he isn't a servant leader, but because he doesn't want to waste his day on a lot of "howdy-doody" time. He is also a celebrity in the Keller-Williams world, so everyone wants to talk to him, take a picture with him, or simply glean advice from him.

Your daily time capsule should be long enough for you to get focused on your projects and take the next action step. That may mean delegating tasks to someone else, or it may be actually taking the action yourself. For example, if you're writing a book as I am doing right now, you'll want to block time to work on that project and to move the ball down the field.

Gary states that high achievers dedicate four hours a day to work on their *One Thing*. Depending on your current situation, you may need to build up to that. But you must carve out the time to work on your most important Priority Projects. This is the time to get focused and figure out what the next action step is.

I started Phenomenal Products by writing a few manuals that took a long time to create. The "problem" was that I had to be at my office at 7:30 a.m. to let the crews in at my service company. So, I got up at 4 o'clock every morning so I could consistently invest at least two hours each day into those manuals. Do you think that investment of time paid off? You bet your bottom dollar it did!

I wrote this book by simply being *consistent.*

PERSISTENCE

Zig often said the most important quality a person can have after character and integrity is *persistent consistency.* Consistency means that you act every day. Persistence means you up your game every day. Tweak your process. Get better at what you do. Being persistent means doing it better each time.

Applying persistent consistency in the right things over a long period of time reaps phenomenal rewards. If you eat right and exercise every day over a period of years, you will be super healthy. If you read the Bible every day for thirty-five years, you'll know the Word of God. If you invest $500 per month from age 30 to age 70 at 5 percent interest, you'll have almost a million dollars.

The same is true if you do the wrong things consistently.

If you consistently fail to implement healthy habits, your health report will show it. If you continue to use credit cards to finance things you can't afford, you'll see the negative result. If you continue to fail to implement the most important things in life and business, one day you'll wake up to a nightmare rather than your dream.

No one can predict what trouble will come our way, whether it be weather related, economy related, or a family issue—but we *can* choose how to respond. Do the best you can with the hand you've been dealt. That's success.

The late Peter Drucker, organizational development expert, said that an organization can only be successful if three things are in place. I think this goes for individuals as well:

1. **Assumptions.** Assumptions come from your beliefs. Are your assumptions correct? Can you reach that goal?

2. **Strategies.** A strategy is the way you do something. For example, if you swing a golf club the wrong way, you're unlikely to hit the ball correctly, and you may miss it altogether! Yes, the assumption is you can play a great round of golf, but not if you don't learn the right strategy.

3. **Discipline.** You can have the right assumptions and the right strategy, but if you don't work hard, you won't get there.

PROCRASTINATION

The first time I shared the *Principles of Phenomenal Performance* in a speech was the opening of one of my Inner Conferences that I hold in association with Ziglar. There's a huge Ziglar focus at that conference, and many of the Ziglar Legacy Certified Trainers are in the audience.

As I was planning that presentation, a sobering thought hit me like a bucket of ice-cold water. I began to think back to the first time I met Zig at a huge conference. I asked one of his associates, who was working the conference with him, how I might establish a relationship with Ziglar. He told me that I could become a distributor of Ziglar products. That made sense to me, and I intended on following up with Ziglar soon after that, but I failed to schedule that meeting for *five years!*

I began to think of all the things I would have lost as a result of simply overlooking an opportunity. It hit me hard as I thought about all the people I would have never met as a result. I thought about all the experiences I would have missed if I failed to implement a simple phone call.

What if I had never made that call? I wouldn't have traveled the world with Tom, helping thousands of people. I would not have had the amazing friendship with him that I have. I would not have had the opportunity to mentor his daughter, Alexandra, who is also one of my best friends in the whole world. To see her grow personally and professionally has been one of the most meaningful things in my life.

I would have lost the opportunity to meet Brenda Sell Jones. Senior Grandmaster Brenda J. Sell is one of our most prominent Inner Circle Members who is the highest-ranking American female in Tae Kwon Do in the world. She is also the most godly woman I know. Her husband passed away, and I had the opportunity to help save her martial arts training and certification business. Our community walked through breast cancer with her, and saw her healed. Not only that, Brenda Sell married my coach Rick Jones and I was the best man at their wedding. Brenda Sell Jones and Rick pray for me on a regular basis and continually pour wisdom into my heart.

I would have missed all of that.

I would not have met Cheri Perry, Inner Circle's greatest advocate. She facilitates several PODS every week and doesn't charge me a penny! She also participates in at least two of my PODS. She travels to every event we have and joins every program I offer. Where would our community be without Cheri Perry?

I would have never met Michelle Prince who inspired this book—the person who kept the dream alive of bringing back Zig Ziglar's *Born to Win* seminars; the person who emcees all of my conferences at no charge!

I would have missed the opportunity to know Nick and Jamie Hallas, who bring their six children to my conferences, and to see those precious kids recite, "I am born to win, designed for accomplishment, engineered for success, and endowed with the seeds of greatness. After all, God don't make no junk! I am a phenomenal product, created to do phenomenal things and to have a phenomenal life."

I would have missed the opportunity to teach Zig Ziglar's I CAN course and the Ziglar Youth Training at my Destin Retreat and see all the kids begin to understand their value.

As I took the stage that day, I almost came to tears as I looked around the room and realized that half of the audience came from my relationship with Ziglar.

In fact, I probably wouldn't even be writing this book right now if I had not made that simple call to Ziglar. Just look at all I would have *lost* by not taking the simple action of following up with Zig Ziglar.

In my book *Discover Your Phenomenal Dream Life,* I share that I almost quit Phenomenal Products at one point. I was discouraged. I didn't understand my potential. I didn't believe the picture, and I didn't know my purpose. I didn't have the right people around me. I didn't have the best plan. I was productive, but not getting the results I wanted.

Look at all I would have *lost* had I quit!

One of the greatest human motivators is the *fear of loss.* If you find yourself procrastinating, take a moment to think about what you will lose if you don't implement. When you find yourself procrastinating, think about your dream for a moment. Are you willing to just let it slip away? Does your dream really compel you? Does it *really* compel you? Check your belief systems. Are you living by the right principles? Are you plugged into the people who can help you?

What will *you* lose if you don't implement?

PROBLEMS

I've found that major life events like a death or a divorce can distract people for long periods of time and cause major drift. It is certainly understandable, but your purpose does not end when someone dies. It only ends when *you* die. God's plan for your life is still valid even if someone leaves you.

Good things can distract us as well. Weddings, graduations, new business opportunities, and growth. Stay focused. Remember your potential. Rekindle the picture. Reconnect with your purpose. Stay plugged into your people. Keep planning and prioritizing what's important now. We tend to stay on the road of distraction too long. Keep using your proven processes and stay positive and productive.

Failure is required for success. You will always have problems, you will always face obstacles, and you will always meet with failure. But as Zig reminds us, "Failure is not a person. It's an event. Yesterday really did end last night. Today is a brand-new day."

PAIN

At some point in the future, you'll say, "I wish I had," or "I'm glad I did." For me, I'm certainly glad I did! As Jim Rohn said, "We must suffer one of two pains: the pain of discipline or the pain of regret. The difference is discipline weighs ounces, while regret weighs tons." Pain is required for success. You cannot be phenomenally successful without pain. You cannot achieve phenomenal performance without pain.

ACTION STEPS

1. Commit to the *Daily Time Capsule* every day except your rest day.

2. Go to page 153 in your *Ziglar Personal Performance Planner* and fill in the Monthly Activity Record. Be sure to list the *Priority Activities*.

3. Go to page 180 in your *Ziglar Personal Performance Planner* and begin outlining the next year.

4. Participate in your weekly POD.

Those who work their land will have
abundant food, but those who chase
fantasies will have their fill of poverty.
—PROVERBS 28:19 NIV

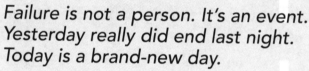

We must suffer one of two pains: the
pain of discipline or the pain of regret.
The difference is discipline weighs
ounces, while regret weighs tons.
—JIM ROHN

Failure is not a person. It's an event.
Yesterday really did end last night.
Today is a brand-new day.
—ZIG ZIGLAR

Don't live your life by circumstance. Instead,
live your life according to a vision.
—HOWARD PARTRIDGE

Lazy hands make for poverty, but diligent hands bring wealth.
—PROVERBS 10:4 NIV

A locomotive is free, but if it's off the tracks it can't go anywhere.
—ZIG ZIGLAR

Vision without action is a daydream. Action without vision is a nightmare.
—JAPANESE PROVERB

Your future success is determined by your daily agenda.
—JOHN MAXWELL

CHAPTER ELEVEN

PRINCIPLE 9: THE PROGRESS PRINCIPLE

Tracking Your Progress **ILLUMINATES** Phenomenal Performance

WHAT'S WORKING, WHAT'S NOT?

Have you seen the flight-tracker screen on an airplane? The GPS readout on the screen shows the route you are about to take and during the flight, it shows you how far you have to go, and how much time it will take to get there.

This is exactly what we need to do when it comes to our goals. In the Planning Principle, I mentioned that you want to identify your "someday goal" and then break it down to a five-year goal, a three-year goal, a one-year goal, a six-month goal, a one-month goal, a this-week goal, and then a today goal.

A short-term goal works the same way. Let's say you want to lose 20 pounds in 90 days. Where do you need to be in 60 days? In 30 days? How many pounds do you lose per week and what is the average per day?

Tracking your performance is simply doing the same thing backward. Just like the flight tracker, you want to monitor your performance. Track it every day. Maybe it's a habit goal. Maybe you want to stop using foul language, or you want to be more positive. Every day you can monitor your progress by counting the number of times you curse or say something negative.

This is what the *Personal Performance Record* in the *Ziglar Personal Performance Planner* is all about. You track your goals in the *My Daily Goals Activity* at the top of the page, track your time in the *My Daily Schedule*, and track your physical activity and your life balance by checking off the eight items at the bottom of the page.

Tracking your progress is extremely important because it *illuminates* your performance, good or bad. For me, the physical activity is one I have to pay close attention to. When my planner reveals, illuminates the fact that I have not exercised for several days, it reminds me to do so. Tracking your goals at the top of the page illuminates whether you are taking action on that goal every day. The time tracker illuminates how you used your time that day.

Pilots are constantly adjusting their direction based on their coordinates. We need to do the same thing in the journey of life and work. Humans can get off track very easily, and we can drift a long way off course without even realizing it. This is a critical factor in phenomenal performance.

Debriefing your activity and accomplishments is also vital for continuous improvement. After every military mission, a debriefing session takes place. What went well? What didn't? What do we need to do better the next day? Our daily mission is the same. We need to debrief every day and every performance and ask those same three questions.

As a speaker and coach, I conduct a lot of presentations, workshops, and conferences. After each and every one, I debrief and ask those three questions. This helps me do it better every time. Every time I hold a conference for our Inner Circle members, many of them compliment us by saying, "This was the best conference yet. We don't know how you continue to do that every time." The reason is that we've done hundreds of events, and we debrief after each one. We also pay attention to what our members need at the time.

I make the trip from my home in Houston to my home in Destin on a regular basis, so I know it takes ten and a half hours door to door with brief stops. Obviously, it takes long if there are more stops, the traffic, and whether I have passengers or pets along for the ride. I can tell you that I have a *goal* of getting there in record time. I don't mind driving; in fact, I would much rather drive than fly personally, but it's a long drive. I'm constantly working on decreasing my drive time and monitoring my performance.

We should always monitor our performance. You want to monitor your daily activity and assess how things are going. Just like my drive to Destin, you have goals with completion dates and many times unexpected events set you back. Perhaps you're traveling the road of life with some passengers, pets, and from time to time there will be events that slow you down, and that's okay. Just don't get sidetracked too long. Get back in the game.

As I mentioned, I was working on this book during my trip to Italy. I planned to write for at least two hours per day and up to three. But every day there was some kind of interruption. People woke up earlier than I expected, or someone saw me on the porch of the Tuscan farmhouse where I was writing and walked up to talk for a while, not to mention the unanticipated slowdown from the time change and the abundance of pasta I consumed, which didn't help with my health goal either!

But Howard, you're on *vacation,* you might say. As mentioned earlier, I don't really do vacations. I relocate! I do a Sabbath rest once a week and for extended periods from time to time. Not only that, but we are out "vacationing" *all* day! So, I like to get some production in every day because I know that's the key to long-term, continued success. As the old saying goes, "Yard by yard, life is hard. But inch by inch, life is a cinch!"

The quality of your planning makes a huge difference, but you have to implement that plan and improve upon it. The debrief of my writing performance in Italy *illuminated* the fact that I could have planned better. I could have left the bed and breakfast in Florence and gone to a café. I could have left the farmhouse in the Tuscany countryside and found a remote place on the castle grounds where no one was likely to find me.

The value in tracking your activity is that you see things *after* the performance that you didn't anticipate. Or you realize you just didn't execute well. Tracking and making adjustments help you perform better in the future. You not only want to take action on your goals every day, but you want to track your progress every day.

You'll notice in the goal-setting process in your planner, that the last step is the completion date. A serious deadline is a powerful force, especially when a cost is involved. Tom Ziglar watched his dad finish many books during his lifetime, and he had just published his first book *Choose to Win*. I wanted our writing group to learn what he had learned through his experiences. One of the participants asked Tom how he finished his book by the deadline. "Simple!" he chuckled. "If I don't get it done, I have to send the publisher their money back!"

If there is a perfect exercise and example of phenomenal implementation, writing a book has to be at the top. The time, energy, and commitment it takes to see a writing project through until the end is incredible indeed. The deadline to complete the manuscript for this book was looming as the Italy trip was ending, so I was thankful to get seven straight hours in on the plane home while everyone else was watching movies. Fortunately, I was able to move the deadline and invest more time in this book than I had originally.

I have a health app on my phone that I sometimes use when I want to be more aware of my daily eating. It counts calories and gives nutritional feedback. Although I understand there is more involved in phenomenal health than just calories, using the app helps me stay on track. Just like a GPS, you have to first put in your current weight and your goal. Each day when I finish logging in my eating and exercise, a statement from the app reads, "If every day were like today, you would weigh...." That's good daily feedback! And guess what? When I use the app, I tend to eat right! When I don't, I don't! So, what's the *one thing* I can do for my health? *Use the app, Howard!*

There are three ways to track your performance. One is to track based on past performance. The second is based on your future goal. The third comes into play when you're in a competition—the score of your competitor!

When my first business was unprofitable and in major debt, I hired consultant Ellen Rohr to help me set up a process to get that business financially healthy. Ellen started her career in the plumbing industry with her husband. They were unprofitable and on the brink of financial ruin when she learned the secrets of being profitable.

They became successful, and she became the first employee for Benjamin Franklin Plumbing. She generated almost $40 million in franchise sales in less than two years. When that company moved the corporate headquarters, Ellen didn't want to move, so she became a very high-paid consultant. We implemented Ellen's financial tracking systems and became very profitable.

Today Ellen is building an exciting franchise operation called ZOOM Drain and coaches exclusively inside our Inner Circle community. How blessed am I? Very.

Ellen likes to track the numbers according to the future budget. She doesn't like me to compare my numbers to last year. She says the past doesn't matter. That's one thing I love about her, but personally I like to make sure I'm beating my previous performance.

If I hit my new goals, which are automatically more than the previous year, then I know I have done that, but there are times when we haven't reached our actual goal, but I'm still above last year. Somehow, I am more motivated knowing that.

You'll also want to track habit goals. Habits are so powerful and supercharged with hidden emotions that we want to be hyperaware of what's happening. Eating habits are a great example of this. You've probably heard that it takes twenty-one days to break a habit. The research done for the book *The Power of Habit* by Charles Duhigg debunks that myth.

It actually takes anywhere from 18 days to 254 days, depending on the emotion tied to the habit. The longer you've had the habit and the deeper it is ingrained in your emotions determines how long it will take. *The ONE Thing* averages this range to 66 days. Many times, professional counseling is required to break a habit.

For maximum performance, you want real-time feedback. Back to the sports team analogy. Imagine playing the full period of the game and not knowing the score. Unfortunately, too many people live like that personally and professionally. It can seem that all of a sudden you wake up and you're overweight. Or you've racked up debt, or let a relationship lapse. Drift is a real problem that can creep up on anyone. Regular tracking fixes that. Regular tracking keeps you accountable and focused.

PHASES

You want to stay aware of how you are progressing, how you are feeling, and how you are thinking. I learned a very powerful lesson from my early mentor that I share in my book *Think and Be Phenomenal.* In fact, the subtitle of that book is *The 5 Levels of Becoming Phenomenal.*

Remember that my definition of success is simply becoming the person you were created to be. My contention is that when you become that person, you automatically do the things you are supposed to do, and therefore have the life you are supposed to have.

I learned from my mentors that we grow into that person through stages or phases, or what I call levels. This is a natural occurrence that everyone goes through when they want to reach new levels in their life or profession.

THE FIVE LEVELS OF BECOMING

There are five levels of becoming: awareness; willing to change; focus; commitment; and character. Let's look at each more closely:

1. **Awareness.** You become aware of a new goal, results, habit, skill, idea, or character trait you want to have.

2. **Willing to Change.** You become willing to face the fear, doubt, criticism, and the work involved to make it happen. This is the step most are unwilling to make, even if they say they want to change. Making a true decision to change causes a lot of fear for many people, and they never get through the fear to get started.

3. **Focus.** You become laser focused on the things you need to do to reach the goal, replace the habit, learn

the new skill, or develop the character trait. But you are just getting started. Focus is incredibly important, but habits change slowly. You still have two major phases to get through.

4. **Commitment.** You become consistent in your new actions. For example, let's say you had a goal to be healthier, and you are consistently eating right and exercising. You're working your plan daily. Even though this is a phenomenal level, what I've found from personal experience and coaching many others is that you're still not there yet. At this point, you have momentum, but if something drastic changes in your life or the perfect storm comes, you can still get off course and maybe never get back.

5. **Character.** This is the level where you've actually become a different person. When you hit this level, you can't do it any differently. You've successfully built a new, positive habit that will move you forward toward your goals.

Habits can be great if we are talking about good ones! In Tom Ziglar's book *Choose to Win—Transform Your Life One Choice at a Time,* he shares this truth: "The fastest way to success is replacing bad habits with good ones."

Do you have habits that are keeping you from reaching your most desirable goals? At every level, we have to observe and evaluate our habits and ask *why* we are doing what we are doing. Remember that habits are developed from your deep-seated, often hidden beliefs. If I say I value health but I eat a quart of ice cream every night before bed, I don't value health, I value ice cream.

You've probably read the following riddle before, but I think repeating it here is a valuable reminder.

WHO AM I?

I am your constant companion.
I am your greatest helper or heaviest burden.
I will push you onward or drag you down to failure.
I am completely at your command.
Half of the things you do can be turned over to me
and I will do them quickly and the same every time.
I am easily managed; you must be firm with me.
Show me exactly how you want something
done and after a few lessons,
I will do it automatically.
I am the servant of all great people, and
of course, of all failures as well.
Those who are great, I have made great.
Those who are failures, I have made failures.
I am not a machine though I work with the precision of a
machine plus the intelligence of a person.
You may run me for profit or run me for
ruin—it makes no difference to me.
Take me, train me, be firm with me, and I
will place the world at your feet.
Be easy with me and I will destroy you.
Who am I?
I am Habit.

Habits are powerful and can be our biggest challenge or our greatest asset depending on whether the habit serves our vision or not.

In his phenomenal book *The Power of Habit,* Charles Duhigg points out that a habit has three parts: First, there is a trigger; then the routine; and third, the reward. The way to replace the habit is to change the routine. The trigger comes and instead of eating ice cream or smoking a cigarette, you go for a walk. The reward is so much better too! But before you can even notice the trigger, you must become aware of it. In order to change your beliefs, you must become aware of them.

Please remember that to change a bad habit, you need support, encouragement, and accountability from others to replace the habit with a good one. This is where it's vital to have the right people around you.

As you track your progress, the real agendas hidden in your soul will be illuminated. Tracking your progress brings awareness. As my good friend Dr. Robert Rohm likes to say, "You can't *BEware* of something until you are *Aware* of something!" Simply discover the agendas that are hidden in your soul. When you observe and evaluate your habits and are willing to change, you can change for the better using the principles in this book.

ACTION STEPS

1. Make sure you are diligently tracking your performance using the *Personal Performance Record* in your *Ziglar Personal Performance Planner.*

2. As you complete a goal, write it in the blanks in the *Charting My Progress* section, beginning on page 183 of your *Ziglar Personal Performance Planner.*

3. Participate in your weekly POD and renew your membership.

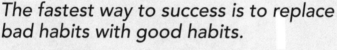

The fastest way to success is to replace bad habits with good habits.

—TOM ZIGLAR

You can't BEware of something until you are Aware of something!

—DR. ROBERT ROHM

CHAPTER TWELVE

PRINCIPLE 10: THE PATIENCE PRINCIPLE

Exercising Great Patience **INCREASES** Phenomenal Performance

WHAT WILL YOU GIVE?

Phenomenal Performance doesn't happen overnight, it happens over *time*. Patience is required for long-term success. Remember that values change slowly and good habits take time to develop. Keep in mind that increasing your performance takes time. Be patient with yourself. You can't expect your habits to immediately change when they have been ingrained all your life, or at least most of your life. Likewise, you can't expect your beliefs to change immediately. It happens over time. Remember the five phases you go through: awareness; willing to change; focus; commitment; character.

Brenda Jones—aka Senior Grandmaster Brenda J. Sell, the highest-ranking female in Tae Kwon Do world—reminds us that a black belt is simply a white belt that never quits. You will experience pain, frustration, letdowns, and roadblocks on the way to mastery. You will want to quit. When you understand that phenomenal performance in any field takes time, you'll have more patience.

Like Brenda, dogged determination puts you in a league of your own. Most people won't exercise the patience required for mastery. We live in an instant-gratification society. We tap our foot in front of the microwave!

But masters understand grit. They understand that patience increases phenomenal performance bit by bit. Line by line. Precept by precept. Little by little. When you practice the fundamentals of thinking right, remember who you are, and Whose you are, remembering your dream, living on purpose, keeping the right people around you, diligently planning, and staying focused on your highest priorities, you will reach your goals. Also using simple systems that save you time, energy, and money, committing to massive action every day, and continuously tracking your progress will move you forward. But now you just need one last ingredient...patience, my friend. Patience.

PUMP

One of my favorite Zig stories demonstrates the principles we have talked about in this book perfectly. It's the story of his famous water pump. Here's the story in Zig's words:

One of the props I use in my talks around the country is an old-fashioned, chrome-plated water pump. I personally love the story of the pump because to me it represents the story of America, the story of the free enterprise system, and the story of life. For your benefit, I hope you've had the opportunity of using one of these old-fashioned water pumps on at least one occasion. That experience will help you to appreciate the significance of this series of thoughts.

Several years ago, two friends of mine, Bernard Haygood and Jimmy Glenn, were driving in the South Alabama foothills on a hot August day. They were thirsty, so Bernard pulled behind an old abandoned farmhouse with a water pump in the yard. He hopped out of the car, ran over to the pump, grabbed the handle, and started pumping. After a moment or two of pumping, Bernard pointed to an old bucket and suggested to Jimmy that he get the bucket and dip some water out of a nearby stream in order to "prime" the pump. As all pumpers know, you must put a little water *in* the top of the pump to "prime" the pump and get the flow of water started.

In the game of life, before you can get anything *out*, you must put something *in*. Unfortunately, there are many people who stand in front of the stove of life and say, "Stove, give me some heat and then I'll put some wood in you."

Many times the secretary comes to the boss and says, "Give me a raise and then I'll start doing better work and being more conscientious." Often the salesman goes to the boss and says, "Make me the sales manager and I'll really show you what I can do. It's true I haven't done much until now, but I need to be in charge in order to do my best work. So just make me the boss and then watch me go." Many times the student says to the teacher, "If I take a bad grade home for this semester my folks will really lay it on me. So Teacher, if you will just give me a good grade this quarter, I promise I'll study real hard the next quarter."

My experience has been that it doesn't work that way. If it did, I could easily imagine a farmer praying, "Lord, if you will just give me a crop *this* year, I promise to plant the seed and work hard *next* year." What they are really saying is, "Reward me and then I'll produce." But life doesn't work that way. You must first put something into life before you can expect to get anything out of it. Now, if you'll just transfer this knowledge to the rest of your life, you can solve many of your problems.

The farmer must plant his seed in the spring or summer before he reaps the harvest in the fall. He also "puts in" lots of work before the crop reaches the harvest stage. The student puts in hundreds of hours of work before he acquires the knowledge and the graduation certificate. The secretary of today who is the office manager of tomorrow puts a considerable amount of extra into her job. The athlete of today who becomes a champion of tomorrow "puts in" a great deal of himself in the form of sweat and effort before he reaps the champion's reward. The junior executive of today who becomes the corporate president of tomorrow is that individual who put himself into the job. The salesman of today who becomes the sales manager of tomorrow is the person who understands the principle of priming the pump. When you put something "in," the law of compensation says you'll get something "out."

Well, let's get back to my friends in South Alabama. South Alabama is hot in August and after a few minutes of pumping, Bernard worked up a considerable sweat. At that point, he started asking himself just how much work he was willing to do for that water. He was concerned about the amount of reward he would receive for the amount of effort expended.

After a time he said, "Jimmy, I don't believe there's any water in this well." Jimmy replied, "Yes, there is, Bernard; in South Alabama the wells are deep and that's good, because the deep well produces the good, clean, sweet, pure, best-tasting water of all." Jimmy is also talking about life, isn't he? The things we have to work for are the things we appreciate most.

That which is easily obtained is generally not worth a great deal. If you could become an MD in a six-week summer course, just how much would it be worth? If you could become a super salesman by listening to a four-hour sales lecture, competition would be so intense your commission would be considerably smaller. Go down the list and you'll discover that those skills and objectives that require your blood, sweat, and tears are the ones that bring the real satisfaction and rewards. Back to the pump.

By now Bernard was getting hot and tired, so he threw up his hands and said, "Jimmy, there just isn't any water in this well." Jimmy quickly grabbed the pump handle and kept pumping as he said, "Don't stop now, Bernard; if you do, the water will go all the way back down and then you'll have to start all over again." That, too, is the story of life. There isn't a human being in existence, regardless of age, sex, or occupation, who doesn't occasionally feel he might as well "stop pumping" because there isn't any water down there. So if you occasionally feel that way, it should be comforting to know that you've got lots of company.

Now let's look at something intriguing and obvious. There's no way you can look at the outside of a pump and determine whether it will take two more strokes or two hundred more to bring forth the water. There's often no way you can look into the game of life and determine whether or not you'll get the big break tomorrow or whether it will take another week, month, year, or even longer.

This I do know beyond any reasonable doubt. Regardless of what you are doing, if you will pump long enough, hard enough, and enthusiastically enough, sooner or later the effort will bring forth the reward. I also know that just as you add nothing to the score if you stop on third base, you can't quench your thirst with the water that almost comes out of the pump. Fortunately, once the water starts to flow, all you have to do is keep some steady pressure on the pump, and you'll get more water than you can use. This is the story of success and happiness in life.

The message is clear. Whatever you're doing, work at it with the right attitude and the right habits, but above all, keep at it with bulldog tenacity and persistence. Just as the flow of water is often one stroke away, the sweet taste of success and victory is often just over the hill or around the corner. Whether you're a doctor, lawyer, student, housewife, laborer, or salesperson, once you get the water flowing, it's easy to keep it flowing with a little steady effort.

We will never know how many youngsters missed winning a college scholarship because they didn't study just 10 minutes more every day. Or how many employees missed out on a promotion because they didn't stay at their task just a few more minutes each day for a few more weeks. Or how many sales were missed because the prospect wasn't given just one more reason to make a yes decision today.

I believe the story of the pump is the story of life and the free enterprise system. I say this because it has nothing to do with age or education, whether you are black or white, male or female, overweight or underweight, extrovert or introvert, or whether you are

Catholic, Jew, or Protestant. It has everything to do with your God-given rights as a free person to work as long as you wish, as hard as you wish, and as enthusiastically as you wish to get everything in life you really want.

As you move to the top, remember the story of the pump. If you start pumping casually or half-heartedly, you will pump forever before anything happens. Pump hard to begin with and keep it up until you get that water flowing. Then a great deal will happen. Once the flow of water starts, just maintain that steady pressure, and the time will come when the rewards will be so enormous that you'll be getting what you want instead of having to want what you have. (Excerpt from *See You at the Top,* Pelican Publishing Company, 1974)

The lessons I personally take from this story:

1. You have to prime the pump. You have to put something in before you get something out. As Jesus said, "Give, and it will be given back to you, pressed down, shaken together and running over."

2. You have to pump like crazy. In others words, you have to work hard to get a small return in the beginning.

3. You have to be patient. You believe that sweet, cool, refreshing water is down there. Don't stop!

4. The reward will be worth it. Once the water is flowing, you just need a little steady pressure on that

handle to keep the flow. It's hard in the beginning, but it gets easier once everything is in place.

As the old saying goes, "Good things come to those who wait." What are you willing to give? How long will you pump? Is the reward you want worth the wait? Is it worth the investment? If not, you need a new picture.

- Consider whether you've accepted the principles required for phenomenal performance.

- Consider whether you're willing to change.

- Consider your commitment level.

- Consider the benefits of being proactive living out these principles in your life and business.

- Consider how you will continue to participate with others.

- Consider participating in a POD to keep these principles alive in your life and business.

- Consider facilitating a POD yourself. Start a POD with your employees, coworkers, church group, or nonprofit group. That will not only help others implement the things they want in their life, but there is nothing that will help you stay on track more than helping someone else. Remember Zig's favorite quote: "You can have everything you want in life if you will just help enough other people get what they want."

Here are the 10 Principles of Phenomenal Performance one last time:

1. **The POTENTIAL Principle:** *Understanding Your Potential Impacts Phenomenal Performance.* "Who do you think you are?" All humans suffer from a poor self-image to one degree or another. Who you think you are, and whose you think you are determines whether you act on your goals or not.

2. **The PICTURE Principle:** *A Compelling Picture Imagines Phenomenal Performance.* "Where are you going?" Human beings do what human beings see in their mind. This can be positive or negative. If you can't see yourself doing something, you won't even try. But when you have a clear picture in your mind, and you believe it, you will take the steps to get there. You have to see the reaching of your goals in your mind first.

3. **The PURPOSE Principle:** *Knowing Your Purpose Inspires Phenomenal Performance.* "Why do you do what you do?" Humans are created for a purpose, but most never find that out. Many live a life that is meaningless, just getting through the stress of the day. Knowing your purpose gives you a new level of energy and passion.

4. **The PEOPLE Principle:** *The Right People Influence Phenomenal Performance.* "Who do you have around you?" The people you have around you will either keep you from being productive or promote your potential and purpose. Your closest friends, family, and associates heavily influence you, whether you admit it or not. Having the right people around you

helps you understand your potential, helps you see a more meaningful picture, and helps you embrace your purpose.

5. **The PLANNING Principle:** *Proper, Focused Planning Initiates Phenomenal Performance.* "How will you get there?" You can't go somewhere you've never been without a map. When you have the right directions, you can get where you are going faster and easier. You cannot even get started without an itinerary!

6. **The PRIORITY Principle:** *Living by Priority Ignites Phenomenal Performance.* "What's important now?" Life offers many opportunities, both good and bad. That's why it is so easy to be distracted. Staying focused on what's truly important every day is key to long-term implementation.

7. **The PROCESS Principle:** *A Simple Process Improves Phenomenal Performance.* "What systems will you use?" Creating simple systems into your life and business makes production more predictable and precise, which saves you time, energy, and money.

8. **The PRODUCTIVITY Principle:** Persistent, Consistent *Productivity Insures Phenomenal Performance.* "What action are you taking?" We need to be more productive to reach goals we have not reached before—and the kind of action we take each day is critical. We need to take *focused* action *every* day that will take us closer to the goal. How

you use your time each day is vital to phenomenal performance.

9. **The PROGRESS Principle:** *Tracking Your Progress Illuminates Phenomenal Performance.* "How are you tracking?" Just like tracking your progress on a trip, you need to track your performance so you know how you are progressing. Are we early? Late? Right on time? Tracking your success reveals, illuminates your performance, good or bad.

10. **The PATIENCE Principle:** *Exercising Great Patience Increases Phenomenal Performance.* "What will you give?" Reaching a level of phenomenal performance doesn't happen overnight, it happens over *time.* The Patience Principle helps you live these principles for the long haul. Diligence over time brings huge rewards.

PASSIVITY

The late Jim Rohn, author and business philosopher, said, "Let others lead small lives, but not you. Let others argue over small things, but not you. Let others cry over small hurts, but not you. Let others leave their future in someone else's hands, but not you." When you are passive, you're allowing someone else to determine your future. Jim Rohn said, "Guess what they have planned for you? Not much!" We have to take personal responsibility for ourselves.

ACTION STEPS

You have to take action.

You have to be proactive.

Give it *all* you've got.

You have *one* life to live.

Live it well!

Live it phenomenally!

If you pump long enough, hard enough and enthusiastically enough, sooner or later, the effort will bring forth the reward.

—ZIG ZIGLAR

A black belt is simply a white belt who never quit.

—SENIOR GRANDMASTER EDWARD B. SELL

Yard by yard, life is hard. Inch by inch, life is a cinch.

—JOHN BYTHEWAY

CHAPTER THIRTEEN

THE POD™ PRINCIPLE

Participating in PODS **IMPARTS** Phenomenal Performance

WILL YOU CONNECT?

In my book *The Power of Community*, I share how I discovered the power of the small group. I now call those groups *PODS*. PODS stands for Power Of Discovery Systems.™

A few years ago, I noticed something at church that would change my life and my future forever.

Every Sunday after church, the members would get in their cars and leave. Many of them seemed to be the same each week. No change, no implementation, no transformation. The sermon was nice, well thought out, and in fact, it was the truth! The problem is that information alone doesn't transform a person.

Then came Tuesday night *home* group. In this setting, the members of the small group all shared. More importantly,

195

they helped each other and intentionally interacted with one another for the purpose of *implementing* what we learned from Scripture.

It was life changing, and it created a sense of *community*. Shortly after that experience, I was introduced to an organization that specialized in small group dynamics. I've learned that implementation happens most effectively in the context of community.

As I shared in The People Principle, we need the support, encouragement, and accountability to become the people we want to be, so we can do the things we want to do, in order to have the life we want to have. I encourage you to read *The Power of Community.* It will help you become the leader you want to be and can transform the way you do life and business, and give you better results.

One of the tools we use to build community, to increase learning, and more importantly implementation is the small group. In a small group, participants have the opportunity to interact to actually *learn* the information; more importantly, they are more likely to implement because of a phenomenon I call the *Power of Discovery.*

As participants interact, they *discover* what they need to do rather than being told. You might say the principles are *caught* rather than taught. When this happens, there is a sense of ownership on the part of the participants, because it appears that it was their idea. Ownership of these principles is very powerful, as they are more likely to be acted on. And in today's "don't-tell-me-what-to-do culture," it is even more vital to create this setting.

Participating in a Growth POD helps you stay accountable to your vision, your values, and the action you should be taking. To join a POD in progress, visit www.HowardPartridgeInnerCircle.com.

I hope you share this book with others so they can reach their biggest dreams and goals. The best way to do that is to host a POD. If you would like to facilitate a POD, I've created a POD for each of the chapters of this book. There are thirteen sessions to perfectly fit a quarterly rhythm, whether it is a church group, business group, or a social club, you can use these POD outlines to facilitate a group.

Anyone can facilitate a POD, but it's key to learn how to be a good facilitator. To learn how to properly facilitate a POD, get my book *The Power of Community* and make sure everyone in your group has their own copy of this book. *Please do not charge for this group session, unless you become one of our certified POD facilitators.* For more information, about becoming a facilitator, please visit www.PowerOfCommunity.com.

PODS

The purpose of the POD is to foster more effective communication. Over time, these groups can move people from a sense of community to a true community experience of belonging and transformation. Unlike what happens in a traditional meeting, in which one person speaks to the group, interaction is encouraged in a POD meeting. These purpose-minded life support groups can be used for almost any reason—to reach company goals, keep a project moving forward, achieve personal goals, change habits, or develop skills or gifts.

Typically including seven to twelve individuals, PODS are designed to allow participants to discover what they need to do, or who they need to become, rather than being taught—or worse, *told*. This is particularly important in today's society because people tend to bristle when you tell them what to do; so, PODS enable team members to discover important concepts on their own. And when they discover something themselves, they feel a sense of ownership, which makes it more likely that they will implement it. When they take action, they do it with a sense of purpose.

In this chapter, you learn why PODS work, what kind of PODS you need, and how to facilitate a Growth POD properly.

Just having small groups is not the answer. Properly *facilitating* the group with a specific purpose in mind is the key to being effective. All too often, regardless of the type of meeting, the leader tends to do all the talking—and this is a mistake. One-way information doesn't transform. To make matters worse, most often the leader isn't a very good speaker!

Even large groups can be organized into many small groups that make up the whole. I learned through my experience in the cell church movement that the largest churches in the world are actually cell churches. In other words, the congregation is organized into small groups that meet in homes, restaurants, or someone's office during the week. After all, how would you get 750,000 members into one church building? Even if you had multiple services, it would be a challenge.

In the book *Community—The Structure of Belonging,* Peter Block suggests that event large groups should break into small groups to *digest* the information that was shared from the stage (my emphasis on *digest*). These groups can also be called "cell groups" or "life groups," that meet on a regular basis to learn and grow together. Every living organism is made up of cells that make life possible.

Military units are organized into squads. One of the most potent of the small groups in the military are the Navy SEALS who eliminated terrorist Osama bin Laden and rescued Captain Phillips from Somali pirates who boarded the U.S.-flagged freighter Maersk Alabama.

If small, interactive groups are so effective, why don't more leaders utilize them? My hunch is that the general population hasn't really thought about it that much, hence the reason for this book and this chapter. I've studied and practiced leadership extensively for a quarter of a century, and I can't think of one single training program that focused on the power of small groups outside of church.

Our culture has a large group mentality that's a hangover from the Industrial Revolution. When we became an industrialized culture, we became an "institutionalized" culture. We simply expect that our institutions will take care of us.

When I started attending church, I didn't question the way it was done until my Tuesday night small group experience. It never crossed my mind until I saw the stark contrast between the small group meeting where ministry was *actually happening,* and someone just doling out information.

Dr. Ralph W. Neighbour Jr. further revolutionized my thinking on this subject. In fact, the first person I remember hearing the word "community" attached to the small group was from Ralph. I learned from him that most institutions are "program based designed" which means they build a "program" that addresses a problem. There's nothing wrong with a program, but the problem is that programs don't solve problems. People do.

Yes, information is important. Yes, inspiration is important. Yes, programs can be effective; but when you have inspiration and information without interaction that causes people to dig deep into their souls and search their hearts, you don't get maximum implementation. And you certainly don't get community.

Even when leaders become aware of the power of the POD, the vulnerability and close proximity of the small group makes their palms sweat. Sitting around a boardroom table at a client's office a few years ago, the owner of the company invited the team to let him know how they truly felt about his leadership effectiveness. It was not pretty. They scorched the man. And frankly he deserved it. But, the bigger point is how he handled it. This was his opportunity to humble himself and seek to understand why they felt the way they did. But he didn't.

Instead, he defended himself and got angry. For the rest of the day, and throughout dinner, all I heard from the man was how his employees were *wrong*. Sadly, that man still has the same culture he had before that meeting. Many leaders are afraid to be vulnerable. They are afraid of the truth. But the truth will set you free to build true community, which imparts the support, encouragement, and accountability you need for phenomenal performance.

It seems like no matter what kind of meeting it is, we have to have a "speaker." As a professional speaker, I'm grateful for that, but why can't we have *less* information and *more* interaction?

More and more, we're going to a so-called *online community* to solve our problems for us. Going to an online community for advice from strangers seems ironic to me since we are more skeptical of others than ever. Is it possible that people go online to get information without having to actually *follow* the advice? Is the appeal of an online community the disdain for accountability? Or is it so we can avoid interacting with real people altogether?

Along with the advice you get from an online community may come insults from people you don't even know—people who don't even use their real name on their social media profile. I personally love interacting on social media because I can network with people, support people, and encourage them, but it is disconcerting to witness cyberbullies who hide behind their screen name.

Growth PODS help you connect in a very powerful way. The best kinds of PODS are face-to-face PODS, but if that isn't possible, the next best solution is video conferencing, where at least you can see who you're talking to. Facial expressions and body language speak loudly. Even though this process is very powerful, even online, there is *no substitute* for in-person interaction.

THE POWER OF THE POD

PODS work because they create engagement. The entire premise of my *The Power of Community* book has been about *engagement.* The way the POD meeting is designed creates mandatory sharing. No one is exempt from sharing in a POD, but it is also designed to create ample space for those who haven't totally committed to the idea of engaging in such close quarters as a POD. Over time, the support, encouragement, and accountability should pull any willing person into a sense of belonging. If not, you have the opportunity to find out why they don't want to connect, which will help you identify their concerns.

The following is why PODS are so powerful when they are properly facilitated.

- **Accountability.** Participants commit to implement the things they said they wanted to accomplish. After all, who wants to show up to a group and admit they didn't do what they were supposed to do? No one.

- **Feedback.** Participants receive input from others that helps them succeed. They get congratulations when they succeed. If they fall short, they get the support, encouragement, and accountability to keep trying.

- **The Power of Discovery.** The biggest advantage of a properly facilitated POD is that the participants *discover* how they need to change instead of someone *telling* them what to do. When people discover something on their own, they tend to take ownership for the idea.

- **Character Growth.** When the POD is properly facilitated, over time POD participation members grow. Values are challenged, changed, or validated, and each person has the opportunity to grow into the person each needs to be.

- **Community.** Of course, community is the ultimate benefit, because there is no greater environment to facilitate implementation. Over time, a sense of belonging is created among the participants, when the POD is properly facilitated, and community can eventually be realized.

- **Multiplication.** One of the little-known benefits of PODS is the opportunity for growth and expansion. As I mentioned earlier, PODS are the building blocks for organizing large groups of people. Once you build your first POD, you will then be able multiply that POD by developing your next POD facilitator for your second POD. Then you duplicate that process over and over again. Find out more at www.HowardPartridge.com/PODS.

- **Filters.** A common lament I hear from business owners and managers is, "I can't tell you how many times I told my employees the same thing over and over again!" As a leader, how do you know if you're getting through to people? Of course you can look at outcomes, but isn't that a little late? Instead, we want to get regular feedback. Understanding the growth process is very important.

THE PRECEDENCE FOR THE POD

The idea of small groups is not new; we just got away from them as a culture. The Junto, also known as the Leather Apron Club, was a club for mutual improvement established in 1727 by Benjamin Franklin in Philadelphia. The Junto's purpose was to debate questions of morals, politics, and natural philosophy and to exchange knowledge of business affairs. It was also a charitable organization, which created a subscription public library consisting of their own books.

Evangelist John Wesley sparked a revival in England with his small group methods. The following is an excerpt from D. Michael Henderson's book *John Wesley's Class Meetings—A Model for Making Disciples*:

> The heart of this revolutionary system was a cell group of six to eight people. They met weekly to give an account for their personal spiritual growth, according to the rules and following the procedures, which Wesley had carefully crafted. The class meeting proved to be such an effective tool for radical personal change that it can be acknowledged as the pivotal element of the Methodist Movement.

This movement became what we know today as the Methodist Church.

Jeff Sutherland, in his book *SCRUM: The Art of Doing Twice the Work in Half the Time,* shares the almost unbelievable results of impossible tasks being accomplished in a fraction of the time by utilizing small groups.

Jerry Wiles is leading a movement in worldwide missions using a method called *orality* that is revolutionizing the mission field.

Blogger Janet Choi writes in her post "Cells, Squads and Pods: The Future of Organizations is Small":

Think small and you will achieve big things. That's the counterintuitive philosophy that nets Finnish game company Supercell revenues of *millions of dollars a day*. So really, **how do you build a billion-dollar business by thinking small?**

One key is the company's supercell organizational model. Autonomous small teams, or "cells," of four to six people position the company to be nimble and innovative. Similar modules—call them squads, pods, cells, startups within startups—are the basic components in many other nimble, growing companies, including Spotify and Automattic. The future, as Dave Gray argues in The Connected Company, is podular.

What is a connected company? According to The Connected Company website:

> Connected companies are learning organizations, with a culture of experimentation and fast feedback. How do they work? Connected companies are made up of small, semi-autonomous teams, connected by a shared purpose and a common platform that helps them coordinate joint action. What does this mean for leaders? Leaders must get used to less control and creating an environment of clarity, trust, and common purpose.

Growth PODS bring together all three keys of building community—support, encouragement, and accountability—and the previous five steps into one simple structure that will not only help your company be more productive but, more importantly, help your team build community. PODS are the building blocks for expanding a sense of belonging, then a sense of community, and eventually the ultimate goal of true community.

In a lunch meeting with my mentor, the wisest man I know, he warned me that PODS must be experienced not taught, so be sure to download the POD outlines at the end of this chapter.

THE PROCEDURE OF THE POD

The most important thing to keep in mind when facilitating a small group is that you are *facilitating* not teaching. In fact, if you want to be a phenomenal leader and coach, stop telling people what to do and ask more questions. Questions engage people. Sure, even in a POD people are learning, and you may teach, but there's even more time dedicated to the interactive parts of the POD.

Facilitating includes listening and allowing participants to interact as well as helping them discover the concepts themselves so they can own them. Facilitating is leading without teaching. A POD must include at least three people but not more than twelve. Community happens most completely in a group of twelve or less, and ideally seven to nine, depending on the purpose of the POD and the amount of time allotted.

The time allotted for a POD depends on the purpose. For example, a daily check-in POD might be only fifteen minutes, whereas a weekly department POD or coaching POD may be an hour. A weekly team POD might go ninety minutes. Don't go over ninety minutes in a POD and encourage people not to take a break during the POD.

THE PRACTICE OF THE POD

Very important: Make sure you meet in a circle! You'll find that some people are uncomfortable in a POD setting. Vulnerability is *required* for POD participation. While building a sense of community is the very reason you want to form a POD, you may have some resistance eventually, even if you don't have it in your initial POD. Don't be surprised. People are not used to being vulnerable, and that is exactly the problem. A POD is a safe place to share as everything is kept confidential.

You may find someone who wants to sit on the outside of the circle, stand, or they find some way to create some kind of barrier between themselves and the group. This is a sure-fire indicator that this person is uncomfortable in this setting. Be sensitive to this reaction and maybe have a one-on-one meeting with that person later to discuss why he or she feels that way. On the other hand, you cannot operate a POD with someone outside the circle. Everyone must sit in the circle as a group.

Turn off all technology during the POD. A POD is about engagement. The purpose of the POD is to connect. The power of the POD comes from the engagement that takes place. Texting or checking email is not allowed during a POD. Computers are banned during the POD as well.

If your POD requires taking notes and some want to take notes on a device, ask them if they would be willing to either take notes by hand to enter later or put the device on airplane mode. Some PODS will have more information than others. For example, should you decide to use PODS in a team meeting where people need to refer to their notes, or take a lot of notes, you will need more tech involved.

Very important: Regardless of the type of leading, less is more. Share less information to get more implementation. As Jerry Wiles teaches about *oral learning methods,* the goal is duplication of the material. That is, someone could leave the group and effectively share what was learned. That certainly isn't the case in most information-laden meetings. The Orality Network's mantra is "Learn a little, practice a lot, implement immediately."

Liz Wiseman, author of *Multipliers—How the Best Leaders Make Everyone Smarter,* encourages leaders to "Play fewer chips." In other words, we would rather have maximum implementation of a little, rather than share a lot of information that never gets implemented.

Humans have a limited amount of information they can digest at one time. Information overload is a major culprit in disengagement. In your POD, focus only on the wildly important. Trim down to the most important information, and there will be better implementation.

All POD participants agree to keep everything in the POD confidential unless the subject matter is intended to be shared with others. Since some PODS are highly personal, it is important for everyone to agree to confidentiality in advance.

The length of a POD can vary, but typically will be from sixty to ninety minutes. The amount of time dedicated to the information and interaction part of the POD will vary based on the overall time frame of the POD. Always start on time and end on time. Waiting for people to show up to start your POD penalizes those who are on time and trains those who are on time to be late. Ending a POD late demonstrates disrespect. The purpose and power of a POD is to foster a sense of community. Ending late can affect the very purpose you are trying to reach.

Keep in mind that when you are facilitating a POD, you are not a teacher or trainer and you don't even have to have a title or position to lead a POD. Anyone can lead a POD, especially if the information part is preplanned and preprinted so others can read the information beforehand. A POD leader must simply facilitate.

PARTS OF THE POD

Each of the five parts of a POD begin with the letter "I" and is therefore called the 5 I's of a POD:

1. **ICEBREAKER**—Engage each and every participant.

2 **INFORMATION**—Share relevant information.

3. **INTERACTION**—Facilitate a discussion of the information.

4. **IMPLEMENTATION**—Request an action item from each participant based on the information discussed.

5. **INSPIRATION**—Close with something inspirational.

OPENING THE POD

Welcome the group by thanking them for coming. Share why the group has come together. Then begin with the Icebreaker question.

1. Icebreaker

The purpose of the icebreaker is to engage the audience. Some personality profiles are less likely to open up, so the icebreaker helps reserved types to share. It also keeps the outgoing types from dominating the meeting as each icebreaker answer is less than sixty seconds long.

The icebreaker question should be positive. All of your meetings should start on a positive note. Ask a question that can be answered in less than sixty seconds, but avoid questions that can be answered with one word answers such as yes, no, or good.

For this book, the icebreaker questions have already been chosen for you. See *The 13-Week POD Outline*. Answering the icebreaker question is mandatory for every participant. The POD facilitator answers first to model the answer. Then it moves clockwise from there. Remember that your participants will likely follow your pattern, so make sure your answer is a good model to follow.

Make sure your answer is sixty seconds or less. As the facilitator, you are modeling the time frame as well. Make sure each person stays within the time limit. You may want to assign a timekeeper to keep the group on track, especially if you have a lot of outgoing people in your group. Of course, this becomes more important as your group grows. For now, just start with a group of three.

Important: There is no discussion during the icebreaker. Many times when someone shares an answer to the icebreaker question, it triggers a thought in someone else's mind and they have the urge to share the thought. Encourage participants that there will be ample time to share during the interaction time and that the purpose of the icebreaker is for each person to engage, but not to generate a discussion yet. On the other hand, the icebreaker should be fun and not cold or dry.

Therefore, comments of affirmation are encouraged from the facilitator. Since you are running the group, it is appropriate for you to make a short comment, or simply compliment each person as you go around the circle. Once the person immediately to your right has answered the icebreaker, move to information.

2. Information

The second I is about the information that needs to be shared with the group. This is the learning segment that includes the information your group needs to know on this particular occasion. For example, if you're using a POD for your team meeting, the information will most likely be about the progress of the projects that the team is working on. For example, in *SCRUM,* author Jeff Sutherland outlines the SCRUM meeting where the product owner shares the progress of the project they are working on.

If it is a learning POD where the group is learning a specific subject, the group will take in the next block of information required. For example, I have a weekly leadership POD where I teach a group of my coaching members leadership concepts. Sometimes we go through specific training programs where there is a set of teaching materials we follow. Other times, I simply teach what I'm learning, and other times a guest speaker will share.

The information can be shared in any way the facilitator deems best. Presentation slides can be used, stories can be told, a video can be played, or participants can read together like you'll do in your Practice POD. Any teaching method can be used, and it doesn't have to be done by the facilitator. Any participant of the group or even an outside speaker can bring the information piece. How you deliver information depends on what you are teaching and the skill level of the person presenting the information.

The power of the POD comes in the interaction part after the information session. Remember that the *Power Of Discovery* is the key to a *POD*. Powerful, life-changing concepts are usually not *taught*, they are *caught*. Facilitating the discussion after the information is when the power of discovery happens. The purpose of the information segment is to provide *direction* to the discussion that comes afterward. The information session will be fifteen to thirty minutes depending on the length and size of the POD.

A sixty-minute POD will look like this:

- **ICEBREAKER:** 10-15 minutes depending on the size of the group
- **INFORMATION:** 15 minutes

- **INTERACTION:** 15 minutes
- **IMPLEMENTATION:** 10-15 minutes depending on the size of the group
- **INSPIRATION:** 5 minutes or less

A ninety-minute POD simply has more information and interaction time:

- **ICEBREAKER:** 10-15 minutes depending on the size of the group
- **INFORMATION:** 30 minutes
- **INTERACTION:** 30 minutes
- **IMPLEMENTATION:** 10-15 minutes depending on the size of the group
- **INSPIRATION:** 5 minutes or less

3. Interaction

The purpose of the interaction segment is to generate a discussion about the information that was shared. The interaction segment is *voluntary*. Everyone does not have to answer the questions, although it would be a pretty boring POD if no one did. Keep in mind that you likely don't have enough time for everyone to share their response to every question that is asked in the interaction segment, so don't go around the circle like you did with the icebreaker. However, you definitely want people to interact, because this is where the magic happens! That is *if* you do a good job facilitating.

Effective facilitating is a skill that takes time and training. Facilitating doesn't come naturally. You'll want to connect with our community to learn how to become a seasoned POD facilitator. Also be aware that there are some common challenges with facilitating. For example, what do you do if everyone goes silent? How to do you create the right discussion questions? These are legitimate and important questions. Since the power of discovery happens in this segment, it's extremely important to get it right.

The first and most important thing to keep in mind during this segment is that you are *done* teaching! The information segment is *over*. Resist the temptation to teach. In fact, resist making a statement at all. Tap into the power of the question instead.

Phenomenal leaders ask great questions. Asking good questions is *key* to coaching, and as a leader, you are a coach. In fact, if you can't coach well, you can't lead well. Make it your goal to become a good coach rather than a good teacher. A good coach asks good questions.

Why are questions so important? Isn't it because good questions engage people? Isn't it because good questions also make people think? Isn't it true that people will *catch* or *discover* more by asking them questions rather than telling them what to do? Have you heard that selling isn't telling? Isn't it true that when you're holding a POD that you're *selling* a concept or idea?

What happens when you give too much information? Is it possible that information overload is more likely to overwhelm someone making it likely they will implement less if anything at all? Isn't it logical that overloading people with too much information can paralyze them with fear? Have you heard of the "paralysis of analysis"? Did you notice that this entire paragraph doesn't have a single statement but is made up entirely of questions? How will asking better questions help you? Can you see how questions engage and empower the participants of your POD?

So, what does a good question look like? Good questions start with what, how, and why:

- What was something you got out of the information that was shared?

- How are you planning on using the information that was shared?

- Why is that important to you?

Can you see how others in your POD can discover things for themselves as someone else answers the questions?

Important: Resist the urge to answer the question or to move too quickly to the next question! Depending on the group dynamics, you may or may not have a lot of talkers. In some PODS, you have so much interaction that it's hard to bring it to a close. In other situations, you have a quiet, reserved group. A good facilitator has to learn how to handle every situation.

If you have a quiet group and you aren't getting the interaction you want, ask the group to share what they are thinking about. Again, if your group consists of more reserved personalities, you may have this occur.

The other reasons participants may not interact at a high level is because they don't know one another well enough to open up or there may be trust issues or conflict among the team members. On the one hand, the POD is a powerful setting for growth and change, but it may be slow getting interaction. That's okay. You cannot force genuine relationships. They grow over time.

4. Implementation

Many meetings end with no call to action. Many times, people leave a meeting wondering, *What did we decide to do?* In this segment of the POD, each participant will share an action step they plan to take as a result of the POD meeting. This step is mandatory for each person to share. Depending on time, you can allow up to sixty seconds for a response or as little as fifteen seconds for them to make a quick statement.

The purpose of this step is to have the participants verbalize an action step. Verbalizing an action step garners more implementation from them and will also reveal what they have discovered.

5. Inspiration

The final step in the POD is designed to end the POD with something highly encouraging. It could be a simple quote, story, video, or a quick exercise. Choose something uplifting and something that relates to the subject matter of the POD. For example, let's assume you are having a POD with your leadership team around vision, you could quote Helen Keller who was reportedly asked, "What could be worse than being blind?" Her response, "The only thing worse than being blind is having sight with no vision."

The POD facilitator does not have to be the one to relay the inspiration. Someone in the group can do it. If you allow someone else to present the inspiration part, make sure you either know what is going to be shared or have a high level of trust and confidence in the person sharing. The last thing you want to do is end your POD on a questionable note.

A simple, easy way to do this is to simply share a quote and what it means to you as you'll see in the *13-Week POD Outline* found in Appendix A.

THE PRACTICE POD

I was having lunch with my early mentor Bill Beckham, who taught me how to facilitate cell groups, and he urged me to have you practice a POD, because they must be experienced to really understand them.

Therefore, I've created thirteen simple PODS based on the content of this book. If you have a Weekly POD, this outline creates a perfect 90-day rhythm. To get started, you need to invite some participants. You could start a group in your company, at your church, or your social group.

Before facilitating a POD, you should experience a POD first and it would be wise to go through our POD Facilitator Training. Visit www.HowardPartridgeInnerCircle.com for more information.

Each POD participate will need a copy of this book, so insure everyone in your group has a copy before you start your POD. Share the purpose of the POD with them—that you want to practice a new format of meeting together that has the

potential for greater understanding, ownership, and implementation than traditional meeting structures.

The only thing worse than being blind is having sight with no vision.

—HELEN KELLER

13-WEEK POD OUTLINE

Each of the following POD Outlines follows the same format, and each is a sixty-minute POD.

If you are going to facilitate a POD, please download the *POD Facilitator Guide* at www.HowardPartridgeInnerCircle .com.

ICEBREAKER: A question is provided for you for each Icebreaker. A group of twelve participants should take no more than fifteen minutes if each person stays within the one-minute time limit.

INFORMATION: Follow the directions on the POD Facilitator Guide or play the Chapter Points video of Howard teaching the points. Download from www.HowardPartridgeInnerCircle. com. The Information section is designed to take fifteen minutes. Reading the entire chapter will take longer, and we encourage participants to read the chapter before the POD. If they don't, encourage them to read it after the POD. *They should own the book to participate in the POD. The POD Facilitator Guide provides a fifteen minute overview of the material.

INTERACTION: Three questions will be provided for discussion. Remember that the Interaction questions are designed to open a discussion.

IMPLEMENTATION: This question is the same every week. Keep the responses under the one-minute time limit. This part should take less than fifteen minutes.

INSPIRATION: Someone in the group reads a quote from the book and shares what it means to him or her. This can be the facilitator or anyone in the group. Keep this portion of the POD less than three minutes.

INTRODUCTION POD: THE #1 REASON PEOPLE DON'T REACH THEIR GOALS

ICEBREAKER: Why are you interested in this group?

INFORMATION: Follow the directions on the POD Facilitator Guide or play the Chapter Points video of Howard teaching the points. Download from www.HowardPartridgeInnerCircle .com.

INTERACTION:

- How has FTI affected you in the past?
- What is your biggest takeaway from the book's Introduction?
- How could the next twelve weeks being involved in the POD help you?

IMPLEMENTATION: What is one thing you will do differently as a result of this POD?

INSPIRATION: Ask someone to read a quote from the book and share what it means to him or her.

CHAPTER ONE POD: PHENOMENAL PERFORMANCE

ICEBREAKER: How would you define the word *performance?*

INFORMATION: Follow the directions on the POD Facilitator Guide or play the Chapter Points video of Howard teaching the points. Download from www.HowardPartridgeInnerCircle .com.

INTERACTION:

- What is your biggest takeaway from Chapter One in the book?
- Why is performance so important?
- What outcome would you like to change?

IMPLEMENTATION: What is one thing you will do differently as a result of this POD?

INSPIRATION: Ask someone to read a quote from the book and share what it means to him or her.

WEEK 3

CHAPTER TWO POD: PHENOMENAL PRINCIPLES

ICEBREAKER: Please share your dominant thought about FTI so far.

INFORMATION: Follow the directions on the POD Facilitator Guide or play the Chapter Points video of Howard teaching the points. Download from www.HowardPartridgeInnerCircle .com.

INTERACTION:

- What is your biggest takeaway from Chapter Two in the book?
- Why is belief so important?
- Share a time when faith improved your performance or fear impaired your performance.

IMPLEMENTATION: What is one thing you will do differently as a result of this POD?

INSPIRATION: Ask someone to read a quote from the book and share what it means to him or her.

CHAPTER THREE POD: THE POTENTIAL PRINCIPLE

ICEBREAKER: How would you define "self-image"?

INFORMATION: Follow the directions on the POD Facilitator Guide or play the Chapter Points video of Howard teaching the points. Download from www.HowardPartridgeInnerCircle.com.

INTERACTION:

- What is your biggest takeaway from Chapter Three in the book?
- Why is self-image so important?
- Share how a low self-image has impacted your performance.

IMPLEMENTATION: What is one thing you will do differently as a result of this POD?

INSPIRATION: Ask someone to read a quote from the book and share what it means to him or her.

CHAPTER FOUR POD: THE PICTURE PRINCIPLE

ICEBREAKER: Do you have a compelling picture for your life? If so, please share it.

INFORMATION: Follow the directions on the POD Facilitator Guide or play the Chapter Points video of Howard teaching the points. Download from www.HowardPartridgeInnerCircle .com.

INTERACTION:

- What is your biggest takeaway from Chapter Four in the book?

- What area of your life do you need a more compelling picture and why?

- How will you get a more compelling picture of your life or work?

IMPLEMENTATION: What is one thing you will implement as a result of this POD?

INSPIRATION: Ask someone to read a quote from the book and share what it means to him or her.

CHAPTER FIVE POD: THE PURPOSE PRINCIPLE

ICEBREAKER: *Why* do you do what you do?

INFORMATION: Follow the directions on the POD Facilitator Guide or play the Chapter Points video of Howard teaching the points. Download from www.HowardPartridgeInnerCircle .com.

INTERACTION:

- What is your biggest takeaway from Chapter Five?
- Why is purpose so important?
- Share a time when you realized you were called to something?

IMPLEMENTATION: What is one thing you will do differently as a result of this POD?

INSPIRATION: Ask someone to read a quote from the book and share what it means to him or her.

CHAPTER SIX POD: THE PEOPLE PRINCIPLE

ICEBREAKER: Name someone who has had a positive influence in your life.

INFORMATION: Follow the directions on the POD Facilitator Guide or play the Chapter Points video of Howard teaching the points. Download from www.HowardPartridgeInnerCircle.com.

INTERACTION:

- What is your biggest takeaway from Chapter Six?
- Why is having the right people around you so important?
- Who do you need to surround yourself with and why?

IMPLEMENTATION: What is one thing you will do differently as a result of this POD?

INSPIRATION: Ask someone to read a quote from the book and share what it means to him or her.

CHAPTER SEVEN POD: THE PLANNING PRINCIPLE

ICEBREAKER: Are you a natural planner? Explain.

INFORMATION: Follow the directions on the POD Facilitator Guide or play the Chapter Points video of Howard teaching the points. Download from www.HowardPartridgeInnerCircle .com.

INTERACTION:

- What is your biggest takeaway from Chapter Seven?

- Why is planning so important?

- Share a time when you really had to commit to a plan.

IMPLEMENTATION: What is one thing you will do differently as a result of this POD?

INSPIRATION: Ask someone to read a quote from this book and share what it means to him or her.

CHAPTER EIGHT POD: THE PRIORITY PRINCIPLE

ICEBREAKER: What would you say is your top priority in life?

INFORMATION: Follow the directions on the POD Facilitator Guide or play the Chapter Points video of Howard teaching the points. Download from www.HowardPartridgeInnerCircle.com

INTERACTION:

- What is your biggest takeaway from Chapter Eight?
- Why is living by priority so important?
- Share a time when you got distracted and what it cost you.

IMPLEMENTATION: What is one thing you will do differently as a result of this POD?

INSPIRATION: Ask someone to read a quote from the book and share what it means to him or her.

CHAPTER NINE POD: THE PROCESS PRINCIPLE

ICEBREAKER: Are you naturally systematic, or are you more spontaneous? Explain.

INFORMATION: Follow the directions on the POD Facilitator Guide or play the Chapter Points video of Howard teaching the points. Download from www.HowardPartridgeInnerCircle .com.

INTERACTION:

- Why is having simple processes so important?
- How will simple systems help you perform better?
- What systems do you need to install in your life or business?

IMPLEMENTATION: What is one thing you will do differently as a result of this POD?

INSPIRATION: Ask someone read a quote from the book and share what it means to him or her.

CHAPTER TEN POD:
THE PRODUCTIVITY PRINCIPLE

ICEBREAKER: How would you rate your daily productivity?

INFORMATION: Follow the directions on the POD Facilitator Guide or play the Chapter Points video of Howard teaching the points. Download from www.HowardPartridgeInnerCircle .com.

INTERACTION:

- What needs to change in your daily productivity?
- How will consistent productivity help you reach your goals?
- Why is consistent productivity important to you?

IMPLEMENTATION: What is one thing you will do differently as a result of this POD?

INSPIRATION: Ask someone to read a quote from the book and share what it means to him or her.

CHAPTER ELEVEN POD: THE PROGRESS PRINCIPLE

ICEBREAKER: What progress have you made since you started this POD?

INFORMATION: Follow the directions on the POD Facilitator Guide or play the Chapter Points video of Howard teaching the points. Download from www.HowardPartridgeInnerCircle.com.

INTERACTION:

- What is your biggest takeaway from Chapter Eleven in the book?

- What do you track consistently?

- What do you have trouble keeping up with?

IMPLEMENTATION: What is one thing you will do differently as a result of this POD?

INSPIRATION: Ask someone to read a quote from the book and share what it means to him or her.

CHAPTER TWELVE POD: THE PATIENCE PRINCIPLE

ICEBREAKER: Share a time when you had to exercise great patience.

INFORMATION: Follow the directions on the POD Facilitator Guide or play the Chapter Points video of Howard teaching the points. Download from www.HowardPartridgeInnerCircle.com.

INTERACTION:

- What is your biggest takeaway from Chapter Twelve?

- What are the benefits of exercising patience?

- What one area do you need to exercise more patience?

IMPLEMENTATION: What is one thing you will do differently as a result of this POD?

INSPIRATION: Ask someone to read a quote from the book and share what it means to him or her.

APPENDIX B

PHENOMENAL PRODUCTIVITY BOOKS

Now that you know *why* you don't implement the things you know you need to implement to have the performance you want, and you understand the principles to live by, you're ready to take advantage of maximum productivity!

The following short list of books are ones that have helped me in the area of productivity and implementation.

These books will reinforce your habits and impart even more wisdom on performing at the highest level possible.

When it comes to learning, more is more. The more you learn about this subject and the more you keep it on your mind, the more likely you will be to adopt the principles.

- *Choose to Win—Transform Your Life, One Simple Choice at a Time* by Tom Ziglar

- *The ONE Thing—The Surprisingly Simple Truth Behind Extraordinary Results* by Gary Keller and Jay Papason

- *Eat That Frog—21 Great Ways to Stop Procrastinating and Get More Done in Less Time* by Brian Tracy

- *The Power of Habit—Why We Do What We Do in Life and Business* by Charles Duhigg

- *Today Matters—12 Daily Practices to Guarantee Tomorrow's Success* by John C. Maxwell

- *The 4-Hour Workweek—Escape the 9-5, Live Anywhere, and Join the New Rich* by Timothy Ferriss

- *The 4 Disciplines of Execution—Achieving Your Wildly Important Goals* by Chris McChesney, Sean Covey, and Jim Huling

ABOUT HOWARD PARTRIDGE

Howard Partridge grew up on welfare in Alabama and moved to Houston at age 18 with only 25 cents in his pocket. He started his first business at age 23 and has transformed it into a thriving multimillion dollar enterprise.

He began teaching his systems and principles to other business owners in 1998; since then he has become the exclusive small business coach for the Zig Ziglar Corporation, a founding member of the John Maxwell Team, and helps individuals, leaders and small business owners around the world reach their biggest dreams and goals.

Howard is president of Phenomenal Products, Inc., which provides training programs for small business owners. He is a prolific writer with *FTI* as his eighth book published in the past five years, each have helped thousands of people to reach their goals by fully implementing his proven-successful principles. He and his wife live in Houston, Texas, and have a home in Destin, Florida.

Visit www.howardpartridge.com for more information.